It Started in Wisconsin

It Started in Wisconsin

Edited by Mari Jo Buhle and Paul Buhle

with an introduction by John Nichols
and an afterword by Michael Moore

VERSO
London • New York

First published by Verso 2011
The collection © Verso 2011
Individual contributions © The contributors

Mari Jo Buhle's "The Wisconsin Idea" appeared in a different form in *Academe*, July–Aug. 2011, republished with the author's permission

Michael Moore's "How I Got to Madison" appeared on his website, Mar. 16, 2011, republished with the author's permission

Tom Morello's "Frostbite and Freedom: The Battle of Madison" appeared in *Rolling Stone*, Feb. 25, 2011, republished with the author's permission

Nick Thorkelson's "What's So Funny 'bout Beer Brats and Cheese and Unions?" appears in another form in *World War 3 Illustrated*, Fall 2011, republished with the author's permission

The moral rights of the authors have been asserted

1 3 5 7 9 10 8 6 4 2

Verso
UK: 6 Meard Street, London W1F 0EG
US: 20 Jay Street, Suite 1010, Brooklyn, NY 11201
www.versobooks.com

Verso is the imprint of New Left Books

ISBN-13: 978-1-84467-888-4

British Library Cataloguing in Publication Data
A catalogue record for this book is available from the British Library

Library of Congress Cataloging-in-Publication Data
A catalog record for this book is available from the Library of Congress

Typeset in Minion Pro by MJ Gavan, Cornwall
Printed in the US by Maple Vail

CONTENTS

Part 1   HOW IT STARTED IN WISCONSIN

INTRODUCTION: WHY WISCONSIN?

By John Nichols

On a bitterly cold Saturday morning in March 2011, I pulled on a heavy jacket and a good pair of gloves and headed south of my hometown of Madison, Wisconsin, to meet some farmers. Many had done their chores before dawn and then brought their tractors to the edge of our state's capital.

The winds were blowing so hard that my daughter, Whitman, and I could barely hear my friend Joel Greeno, a dairy farmer from the far western part of the state, when he shouted: "Let's roll." Greeno had put out the call to members of the Family Farm Defenders and Wisconsin Farmers Union to assemble that day. Fifty tractors fired up and began the three-mile ride into Madison. As we rounded the first corner onto one of the city's major thoroughfares, a small group of children held up signs reading: "Thank you, farmers!"

As our farm parade got closer to town, a larger crowd unfurled a banner that declared: "Workers and Farmers Pull Together!" The crowds grew larger and larger. Passing cars and buses honked their horns in the rhythmic cadence of a movement battle cry: "This is what democracy looks like"—*beep, beep, beep, beep, beep, beep, beep, beep, beep.* Drivers rolled down their windows and shouted: "Thank you! Thank you!" When our tractorcade pulled up the hill and into the great square around the capitol, 150,000 Wisconsinites greeted the farmers with chants of "An injury to one is an injury to all!" and "Solidarity!"

Greeno and the other farmers had come to join the largest pro-labor mass mobilization in modern US history. After Wisconsin governor Scott Walker, a conservative Republican taking cues from corporate donors and right-wing think tanks, moved to eliminate most collective bargaining rights for state, county, and municipal employees and teachers as part of a broad plan to defund public services, Wisconsinites pushed back. The unions that were most threatened may have taken the lead. But they never stood alone.

When schoolteachers in Madison walked off the job to lobby against Walker's bill, they were followed by thousands of students who marched more than two miles to the capitol. When the teachers went back to work, parents stepped up to fill the void. The crowds at the capitol grew from thousands to tens of thousands to hundreds of thousands. Small towns across the state hosted their first-ever labor rallies. Then those who marched in the villages and towns of the state headed to Madison to join the rallies that grew larger and larger, and more and more diverse, as African American and Latino high school students from the urban core of Milwaukee rallied with eighty-year-old farmers from towns too small to find a place on the map.

The Reverend Jesse Jackson, astounded by what he was seeing, told a crowd gathered outside the capitol on a frigid Friday night, "This is a King moment. This is a Gandhi moment." And he was right. The protests in Wisconsin captured national, even international, attention and caused union leaders in the United States, after being so battered for so long, to speak not just of a rebirth of the labor movement but of a renewal of the most fundamental of all radical precepts: solidarity.

But for all its international importance, what happened in Madison and the smaller communities of the state in the first months of 2011, and what continues now, is very much a Wisconsin moment. And this fine collection of essays seeks to put that moment in historical and contemporary, regional, and global perspective.

I know a bit about Wisconsin. My ancestors on my dad's side came to Wisconsin in 1823 to mine lead near Mineral Point. My mom's people arrived a decade later to farm in the Wyoming Valley. I was raised with an outsized regard for Wisconsin, by a mother who made sure we never passed a Wisconsin historical marker without stopping.

So when I say that I have never been prouder of my state than I was during those remarkable weeks in February and March 2011, when hundreds of thousands of Wisconsinites launched mass proworker and prodemocracy protests that would prove to be the largest and most sustained of their kind in the modern history of the United States, it is in this context. And that pride has only grown as public employees, teachers, students, private-sector workers, working farmers, small business owners, and their allies have maintained the momentum—and the broad opposition to Governor Walker's proposals to remake Wisconsin as a more nasty and brutish place.

Nastiness and brutishness have been in ample evidence of late, not just in Wisconsin but across the United States. Walker may have been the first in a new crop of Republican governors to go for it and try to implement the whole of the corporate agenda—as dictated by the billionaire Koch brothers and the array of front groups and putative think tanks they have funded. Even as Wisconsin was fighting back, word came of struggles in Ohio, Michigan, Maine, Florida, and other states. There is really no way to decouple the combat at the state level from the wrestling in Washington over proposals by the same right-wing forces to barter off Medicare to the insurance industry and social security to the speculators on Wall Street. It is, as the great Wisconsin governor and senator Robert M. La Follette said, "the old fight."

"The great issue before the American people today is the control of their own government," La Follette explained in 1912. "In the midst of political struggle, it is not easy to see the historical relations of the present Progressive movement. But it represents a conflict as old as the history of man—the fight to maintain human liberty, the rights of all people."

La Follette believed then, as I do now, that Wisconsin had a unique role to play as a leader in that struggle. Wisconsin, "Fighting Bob" argued, had always led the nation: Striving for higher ideals, asking little and giving much. Wisconsinites fought to end slavery, break up the trusts, and make our state what Teddy Roosevelt called America's "laboratory of democracy."

In early February, as Walker outlined his plan to break the unions, undermine local democracy, and consolidate power in the hands of his elite friends (to the extent that campaign donors can be called friends), it seemed as if the laboratory was producing something toxic—an assault on public servants that would quickly spread from Madison to other state capitals where Republicans were seeking to use fiscal challenges as an excuse to score political points against any unions, environmental organizations, and other groups that might question the purchase and monopolization of our politics by multinational corporations.

But Wisconsinites did not follow the script handed them by

Governor Walker and his out-of-state puppet masters. Wisconsinites pushed back.

Two thousand graduate students and their allies rallied on the Monday after Walker launched his assault on the state's history and values. By Tuesday they were 12,000 or more. By Wednesday, as public school teachers and high school students marched to the capitol, 30,000 people filled the streets of downtown Madison. The demonstrations spread across Wisconsin, from Superior to Kenosha, from Shullsburg to Sturgeon Bay. By that Thursday, Democratic state senators had made real the promise of representative democracy by refusing to allow the enactment of legislation proposed just six days earlier and that the people clearly opposed.

As David Vines, a University of Wisconsin student who joined the protests, said: "This is what the Founders intended." David was right. The people spoke. And the powerful listened—well, at least some of the powerful.

Walker and his legislative echo chamber would finally push a version of their antilabor agenda through the state assembly and senate. The *New York Times* would even suggest that the governor had won. But it was a hollow victory that would be stalled in the courts for months and that would inspire a political pushback characterized by recall campaigns to remove Walker's minions from their legislative sinecures. And, far from crushing the opposition, Walker's power grabs emboldened and expanded the movement against them—drawing that remarkable crowd of 150,000 that greeted our tractorcade on the Saturday after the legislature acted.

Governor Walker may win a battle here, a skirmish there. But he has sealed his fate and that of the agenda handed him by the Koch brothers and their think tanks. The movement that rose up in opposition to that agenda has maintained its momentum in Wisconsin, spread to other states, and been hailed as an inspiration by activists as far away as the Middle East. Wisconsin once more has led, and in the right way, by pushing back, finally, against the limitless demands of a CEO class that will not be satisfied until the great largesse created with the blood, sweat, and toil of the great mass of working Americans is vanquished.

La Follette could not have been clearer about what happens when corporations are allowed to engage in political competition, using their vast resources to warp our electoral processes. "When legislatures will boldly repudiate their constituents and violate the pledges of their platforms, then indeed have the servants become the masters, and the people ceased to be sovereign—gone the government of equal rights and equal responsibilities, lost the jewel of constitutional liberty," declared the great Progressive at the opening of the last century. "Do not look to such lawmakers to restrain corporations within proper limits. Do not look to such lawmakers to equalize the burden of taxation"—or, in any other sense, to do right by the people.

Corporations have become the masters of legislators and legislatures, not just in Wisconsin but across the United States. The US Supreme Court's egregious decision in the case of *Citizens United v. FEC*, which gave corporations free rein to spend as they choose to buy elections, has only made a bad circumstance worse.

There will still be electoral battles to defend democracy. They will play out along broader lines in the months and years to come, thanks, at least in part, to the leadership provided by the people of Wisconsin. That leadership, which is examined and outlined in this fine collection of essays, has taken many forms. Some are rooted in the state's historic traditions, some in its contemporary challenges. But it is important to recognize that Wisconsin is not an outlier state. It is, at its best, a state that reminds Americans of democratic duties that we neglect at our national peril.

Wisconsin has led again in precisely the way that the Founders proposed, and that their truest descendent, Robert M. La Follette, encouraged. James Madison, for whom Wisconsin's capital was named, and the authors of the Constitution and its Bill of Rights, whose names identify the downtown Madison streets that hosted the great protests of 2011, outlined a right to assemble freely and petition for the redress of grievances. Those rights were not imagined, by the Founders or their heirs, as incidental or transitory. They are to be exercised continually. La Follette recognized this when he declared that "democracy is a life." What La Follette meant is that democracy does not end on election day. Democracy begins on election day. It is not an act but an action, and that action—performed not just at the polling place but in the halls of government, not just at the campaign rally but at the post-election protest—is what makes real the promise La Follette made in his day: "The people shall rule!"

A century ago the robber-baron elites heard that promise as a threat. But the people of Wisconsin heard it as a call to action. In response they forged a progressive populist movement that would influence and inspire Franklin Delano Roosevelt's New Deal and the great social and economic progress of the twentieth century.

The "old fight" is on again, as a new generation of robber-baron masters and their servant legislators seeks to undo not just the regulatory and programmatic legacy of the New Deal but of twentieth-century progress. They played their hand first Wisconsin, and they learned the hard way that the people are not so disengaged or so disenchanted that they will easily surrender their rights. When they took to the streets to defend those rights, Wisconsinites gave what Walt Whitman described as "the sign of democracy." And they passed it on to America. Once more, the people are on the march, in Madison, in Lansing, in Columbus, in Augusta, in Tallahassee. In Washington. And if the challenges they face today seem every bit as daunting as they did in La Follette's time, so too does their responsibility. What started in Wisconsin cannot end in Wisconsin. Just as the promise that was made by La Follette a century ago in Wisconsin was passed on to the rest of the United States, so the movement that began in Madison on those cold February and March days must spread. The "old fight" has been joined by a new generation that shares Jefferson's enlightened view regarding "the palpable truth" of the American experiment: "That the mass of mankind has not been born with saddles on their backs, nor a favored few booted and spurred, ready to ride them legitimately, by the grace of God."

Jefferson proposed that the annual celebrations of the founding moment might serve to "refresh our recollections of these rights, and an undiminished devotion to them." But, on this point, La Follette, a borrower from Jefferson on so many matters, got closer to the truth: "Democracy is a life." When we live it to the fullest, at the ballot box and on the Capitol Square, in our ideals and our actions, we edge our states and our nation toward the realization of the shared promise of Jefferson in the eighteenth century, La Follette in the twentieth, and the Wisconsin workers and farmers of the twenty-first: Despite it all, the people shall rule!

ASKED REPEATEDLY WHY HE AND THE WISCONSIN G.O.P. PUSHED SO HARD FOR THE "BUDGET REPAIR BILL," GOV. SCOTT WALKER RESPONDED WITH A SET OF DISINGENUOUS SOUND BITES:

BUT WHEN HE THOUGHT WE WEREN'T LISTENING,* HE USED SOMEWHAT DIFFERENT LANGUAGE:

* DURING THE FAMOUS PRANK PHONE CALL FROM A BLOGGER PRETENDING TO BE RIGHTWING MONEYBAGS DAVID KOCH

© Becca Dilley

2 THE WISCONSIN IDEA

By Mari Jo Buhle

The events in Wisconsin during spring 2011 will long be considered remarkable in many ways. That includes the documenting of the protests. Perhaps at no previous time have so many journalists—paid and unpaid—gathered so much information about a protest movement and dispersed it in so many formats so quickly. Ubiquitous, touching, and often hilarious reporting of the responses to Governor Scott Walker's "budget repair" bill proved to be a key element in the fast-paced events. Internet social media multiplied, including websites, Facebook pages, and Twitter feeds. On Twitter, #wiunion carried commentary minute by minute and provided instantaneous updates on legislative actions and protests inside and outside the capitol. The Wisconsin Wave and Defend Wisconsin, organizations formed to promote progressive values and politics, on their websites and Facebook pages, provided additional outlets for strategizing and calendars of upcoming events throughout the state. The website Uppity Wisconsin: Progressive News from the Cheddar Sphere offered analysis and links to other news sources.

Documentarians captured the newly aroused activist spirit of the prime target of Walker's bill: the public-sector workers who stood to lose many of their collective bargaining rights. Teachers, health-care workers, and correctional officers from around the state filled the streets adjoining the Capitol Square, while parents, schoolchildren, and private-sector union members joined their ranks. Wisconsin boilermakers, sheet-metalworkers, carpenters, and Teamsters, among others, with their union insignias displayed on jackets and banners, gave witness to the state's vital labor history. The occasional chorus of dancing cows (well, people in cow costumes spelling out *solidarity* with the letters across their chests) and one memorable tractorcade led farmers into the fight to preserve workers' rights. Those public-sector workers strategically excluded from the governor's bill, firefighters and police, accompanied a wide assortment of the old and young concerned about the welfare of their state. Out-of-staters, mainly union members from as near as Minnesota and Illinois and as far as New York and California, joined in solidarity and, like uniformed firefighters and Cops 4 Labor, were greeted with cheers: "Thank you, thank you, thank you!" Midwestern politeness to visitors and to people in uniform? Perhaps, but also an expression of pride of place. In addition to publicizing the opposition of all these people to Walker and the Republican legislators, the stories by hundreds of journalists reflected, to a greater or lesser degree, a common theme: "We Are Wisconsin."

At first sight of the crowds circling the capitol, outsiders and visitors might ask: Why were so many demonstrators wearing red jackets and stocking caps? The official state color is blue, but the University of Wisconsin, especially its popular sports teams, known since 1889 as the Badgers, inspired demonstrators to adopt its emblematic cardinal red as the official protest color. Old and young alike donned caps and jackets bearing athletic insignia. Many carried signs or pinned to their coats buttons bearing images of the turtleneck-wearing, strutting Bucky Badger. Rallies, which began with the singing of "The Star-Spangled Banner," moved on swiftly to "On Wisconsin," the university's fight song since 1909 and the official state song since 1959. Occasionally, the bands added the more informal university song, composed by two professors in 1919 and set to a polka beat: "If You Want to Be a Badger, Just Come along with Me." Speakers opened rallies by greeting the crowd with "Hello, Wisconsin!"

No idea figured quite so prominently throughout the course of events as that of the identity of Wisconsin, including its status as the dairy state, the nation's top producer of cheese. The VO5, a Madison funk-rap group, performed the highly original "Cheddar Revolution," a lively song condemning Scott Walker and celebrating the state's democratic heritage as symbolized by its popular dairy product. Solidarity rallies across the United States, Europe, and the Middle East picked up on this imagery. Protesters were decked out in "cheeseheads," a foam hat created in 1987 by the "father of fromage," Milwaukeean Ralph Bruno, to look like a giant piece of gouda-style cheese. Worn by avid

Green Bay Packer fans and protesters in Cairo alike, the cheesehead hat signaled, "We Are All Wisconsin."

Although events in Wisconsin ran concurrently with similar protests in other midwestern states recently captured by the GOP, the turnouts in Madison underscored the state's history and distinctive progressive heritage. On Saturday, March 19, when an estimated 150,000 protesters formed the largest rally in the state's history, wild cheers went up for an unlikely hero: a family farmer. Tony Schultz, born and raised in Wisconsin and the farmer-director of the Family Farm Defenders, an organization promoting sustainable, small-scale agriculture, gave an impassioned speech on the improvised stage in front of the capitol. "What is a union anyway," he asked, "but working people coming together, acting together, to improve their lives?" Standing next to his family, he explained how the schools, the largest employer in small towns, kept struggling downtowns together. Now schools faced their gravest threat with the dismissal of teachers and the evisceration of their educational budgets. He insisted that the governor's plan would erode the public health system and threaten small farmers who could not afford to buy into private insurance plans. In his mind, he said, this struggle was an attempt to hold onto what Wisconsinites had long fought for. "No, Not in MY Wisconsin!" declared one protest sign.

These themes had a familiar ring to Wisconsinites: they evoked the farmer–labor solidarity of the 1910s, a movement that had defeated the corporate interests. Wisconsinites could do it again. Or so third-generation family farmer Schultz insisted, to the roaring approval of the crowd, and soon also to the many thousands who took in his message on YouTube.

Schultz's booming voice echoed the sentiments of other protesters: the new Republican governor's budget bill was, as much as anything else, a monstrous affront to Wisconsinism. The Republican state victory in November 2010 resulted from a combination of public apathy and a sharp disappointment in Democratic leadership, in both the state and the nation. The enthusiasm that swept Barack Obama to victory in 2008 had all but disappeared in Wisconsin, and Scott Walker managed to capture 52.3 percent of the gubernatorial vote. Few anticipated, however, that the heretofore nondescript Milwaukee county executive would act so precipitately (or ruthlessly) as to sweep away a half-century of collective bargaining rights for public employees. Many

Wisconsinites were proud that in 1959 their state, under then-governor Gaylord Nelson, had been the first to enact legislation allowing union representation for public workers. Five decades later they were stunned when, under Walker's leadership, the Republican majority determined to turn back history by stripping state employees of bargaining rights and subjecting what remained of their unions to such limits that they would effectively cease to exist.

Walker and the GOP aimed to undermine legislation that had fed Wisconsin's political identity for much of the past century. Their immediate legislative agenda would devastate social services, including the jobs of teachers and health workers, and overturn a wide assortment of environmental protections. Municipalities, for example, would no longer be required to test their water supplies for impurities; the state would eliminate funding for local recycling programs; the governor could sell off state-owned power plants in no-bid deals; and caps would be raised for the number of students admitted to for-profit online schools, while the authorization of charter schools would pass from locally elected officials to a board appointed by the governor.

Indeed, Walker's repair bill was more of a dismantling bill that would turn half of civil service jobs, spanning fifteen state agencies, into patronage positions filled by appointment by the governor. The measures would, in all, mark a stunning return to the Gilded Age, remembered best for robber-baron industrialists, unchecked political patronage, and unembarrassed corruption.

THE RETURN OF "FIGHTING BOB"

In response, protesters improvised on the state's motto, "Forward," adopted in 1851 to signify Wisconsin's pledge to lead in national affairs, and shouted repeatedly: "Forward, not backward."

Tony Schultz, the family farmer from the little village of Athens, near Wausau, appropriately interpreted the dangers posed to the state's legacy by making himself into a twenty-first-century version of "Fighting Bob," the most admired opposition political figure in Wisconsin history. Robert M. La Follette Sr., who began his term as governor in 1901, emerged as a national symbol of progressivism. Like Schultz, La Follette cherished his rural origins. Born in 1855 in a log cabin in the tiny agricultural township of Primrose in south-central Wisconsin, by his late teens La Follette found himself in the nearby capital city, soon to enroll in the state university. After graduation La Follette decided to become a lawyer, and a growing political ambition prompted him to run first for district attorney in 1880 and then in 1884 for Congress. Although young and relatively inexperienced, he built his successful campaign on two important foundations: an unlimited respect for farmers and workers and his own near-obsession with the idea of efficiency in government.

Inspired by the Granger and Populist movements, which had challenged corporate power, especially as invested in railroads and banks, La Follette garnered wide public support to limit the political influence of corporations and to identify, in the patronage system, the major enemy to economic, social, and educational progress—and to fight the enemy to a standstill, if not vanquish it entirely. All the elements in La Follette's program as governor, in short, complemented its core idea: the purpose of government, first and foremost, was to serve the people.

Self-avowed "La Follette progressives" welcomed the news that reformers were making similar demands in other states but stubbornly insisted that Wisconsin excelled as a "laboratory for democracy." Two-thirds of the population were immigrants or the children of immigrants, many of whom brought their progressive leanings from the Old World. Germans and Scandinavians had volunteered and died in large numbers in the Civil War crusade against slavery. Likewise, socialist impulses had come early and remained in place for generations, especially in Milwaukee, where in 1910 Socialists captured the mayor's office and Victor Berger became the nation's first Socialist in Congress. Isolationist sentiment also had wide support among those Wisconsinites who suspected that it was Wall Street financiers who craved war profits and therefore pushed the nation into war. La Follette and the Progressives drew on these traditions and, outside Milwaukee, came to surpass the Socialists in the collective memory of reform.

Although La Follette left the governor's office in 1906 for the US Senate, the legislation he sponsored at the state level provided national precedents and inspired his Progressive successors at home. "We cannot halt or turn back," he declared, "without bringing disaster to our own state, and discourage all progress along those lines in other states." Many Wisconsinites took pride in his first victory, the primary election law, which established the mechanisms for voters to choose candidates for elections. They also acknowledged his success in achieving an ad valorem tax for railroads and the establishment of the railroad commission. They also attributed to La Follette many other progressive reforms, such as the workers' compensation system and the minimum wage, railroad rate reform and progressive taxation, government transparency, municipal home rule, nonpartisan elections, and the open primary system. Belle Case La Follette, prominent in the women's suffrage movement, ensured that her husband would back granting women the vote. "We cannot have real democracy while one-half of the population is disfranchised," he argued. As one professor emeritus of the University of Wisconsin–Madison recently (if a bit anachronistically) remarked, if La Follette were alive to witness recent events in his state, he would be "standing with the protesters, screaming, 'Right On!' "

As governor-elect Walker quickly cast his dark shadow over La Follette's legacy. It was rumored that Walker deliberately chose an unconventional site for his inauguration ceremony in January 2011. He strategically positioned himself so that the beloved bust of Wisconsin's favorite reformer would be securely out of view of spectators and photographers alike. Little did Walker know that by the middle of February, protesters would be festooning that bust with carnations and roses and carrying signs reading, "La Follette Forever."

Most of all, La Follette symbolized a government pledged, simply, to make life better on the home front. He loomed, almost larger than life, as the timely champion of a host of reforms such as the regulation of working conditions in factories, including the hours worked by women and children; regulation of the insurance industry and public utilities; the promotion of producer and consumer cooperatives; broad public health programs and major conservation initiatives; and tax laws that shifted the tax burden to corporations and the wealthy. As David Obey, a Democrat who retired in 2011 after forty years in the US House of Representatives, put it, La Follette "began to put working people in the driver's seat."

"Fighting Bob" La Follette, backed by farmers and workers, served in the US Senate from 1906 to 1925. He died, reportedly of exhaustion, just months after completing his 1924 presidential campaign for the Progressive Party. While his body lay in state in the Wisconsin capitol's rotunda, an estimated 40,000 people paid their respects. Many of his ideas, including the "brains trust," and some of his slogans reappeared in Franklin D. Roosevelt's New Deal. In Wisconsin the La Follette legacy lived on. "Which shall rule?" La Follette had asked, channeling nineteenth-century state Supreme Court judge Edward G. Ryan. "Wealth or man? Which shall lead, money or intellect? Who shall fill public stations, educated and patriotic free men, or the feudal serfs of corporate wealth?"

The questions that Ryan and then La Follette posed decades ago suddenly reappeared prominently in the demonstrations in February and March 2011, as did two clean-government measures that La Follette's followers had bequeathed to generations of voters, the referendum and (especially) the recall. And it was perfectly in character for latter-day La Folletteites to single out for criticism two of the governor's key financial backers: Charles G. and David Koch (pronounced *Coke*), the billionaire brothers from Wichita, Kansas, who had contributed so generously to Walker's election campaign.

Apparently aiming to make Wisconsin a model for a nation-wide attack upon the "social state," one Koch-backed organization, Americans for Prosperity, set up a branch office barely a block from the capitol, facilitating access to the governor's office. Another organization drawing on Koch financial support, the American Legislative Exchange Council (ALEC), founded in 1973, for more than forty years had been supplying conservative office holders with model legislation designed to protect and enhance corporate interests and were now enjoying success in GOP-led state governments.

In short, the Koch brothers and ALEC reminded concerned Wisconsin citizens of the kind of corporate interference that La Follette had devoted his political career to quashing. "The great issue before the American people today," he noted in 1912, "is the control of their own government. In the midst of political struggle, it is not easy to see the historical relations of the present Progressive movement. But it represents a conflict as old as the history of man—the fight to maintain human liberty, the rights of all people." A century later Governor Walker made La Follette's message all the more poignant. He had not waged an especially strident campaign, but once in office acted with amazing speed to dismantle, almost literally piece by piece, the legislation that marked Wisconsin's distinctive Progressive legacy. But however distressing Walker's agenda for the state, it did not all originate with him. Walker was hardly more than an agent, La Follette probably would have said, for the monied outsiders who had no real interest in the welfare of Wisconsin citizens. One of the most popular messages on protest signs read, "Gov. Walker Is a Koch-Head." Then, on May 7, in true local fashion, protesters organized the Wisconsin Workers' Fishing Opener and Boat Parade to greet Walker as he performed his ceremonial duty on Lake Wissota, near Chippewa Falls, to mark the beginning of one of the state's most important sport seasons.

Protesters chose other corporate targets, too. Union locals, including nurses', firefighters', and boilermakers' unions, organized substantial protests directed at another major Walker backer, M&I Bank, by asking people to withdraw their money. Others asked Wisconsinites to boycott other businesses that helped to fund the GOP campaigns, notably the home improvement retailer Menards, and Johnsonville sausage, maker of bratwurst, one of the state's signature delicacies. The Autonomous Solidarity Organization announced plans for a "people's brat fest" as an alternative to the popular World's Largest Brat Fest, a four-day event held annually over Memorial Day weekend since 1983 and sponsored in part by Johnsonville.

Few could have been surprised, then, when protesters took advantage of another La Follette–backed initiative. As the occupation of the capitol eased, popular committees formed to begin organizing recall elections of all eligible Republican legislators. By Wisconsin law, the governor and legislators are subject to recall only after serving one full year in office. While Walker could not be subjected to a recall vote until early 2012, some Republican legislators, including some of Walker's chief supporters, were vulnerable to immediate recall. And many soon pledged to initiate a recall referendum on Walker himself for January 2012.

The mark of La Follette upon the recall tactic was indelible. Ironically, though, the state GOP usurped for its own rather nefarious purposes one of La Follette's proudest achievements: the open primary. Intending to quash the "menace of the political machine," the Wisconsin legislature in 1904 opened primaries to anyone, regardless of ideology or political affiliation. "Open primaries aren't just part of a political system in the Badger State," one reporter contended, "they're part of a Wisconsin tradition." During the recall elections of 2011, however, the state Republicans used the open primary law not to ensure a democratic process but simply to stall for time and burden Democrats with considerable campaign expenses. They ran fake Democrats as spoiler candidates, in some cases individuals who had served in executive capacities in local GOP organizations. Hardly any Wisconsinites needed help to translate the Twitter-speak shorthand that appeared on protest signs: "WWFBD?"

THE WISCONSIN IDEA

What, indeed, *would* Fighting Bob do? La Follette would surely have cheered the campaign led by public employees' unions, some of which were founded in Wisconsin. He would have welcomed without reservation the participation of students and faculty alike from the state's chief educational institution, the land-grant University of Wisconsin.

La Follette, the first UW graduate to serve as governor of the state, developed during his administration the basic program of the "Wisconsin Idea," the notion that "the boundaries of the University are the boundaries of the state." He prompted the faculty to help legislators improve efficiency and honesty in government. For example, he had UW economist and labor historian John R. Commons draft the state's first civil service law and the nation's first workers' compensation law. "In no state of the Union," La Follette noted in his autobiography, "are the relationship between the university and the people of the State so intimate and so mutually helpful as in Wisconsin." University president Charles Van Hise in 1906 expanded this idea to create the UW extension system, which by the end of the twentieth century had become the state's vast system of public higher education. By the time Walker took office, the UW System comprised twenty-six campuses serving approximately 182,000 students each year and employing more than 32,000 faculty and staff.

At the spring rallies of 2011, speakers invoked the Wisconsin Idea, while protesters at large demanded its defense against the governor's plan to undermine it. For generations UW faculty members had continued to work with state legislators to draft pathbreaking bills, such as the social security legislation that ultimately served as the template for the national program enacted during Franklin D. Roosevelt's administration. Walker, by contrast, looked elsewhere for help in formulating legislation, namely, to corporate leaders and conservative advocacy organizations, and in general began his administration by making the state's public educators his chief adversaries.

Walker's budget bill appeared in February as a frontal attack on public education at all levels. K-12 teachers responded by staging what they called a four-day absence, and an estimated two-thirds of Madison teachers turned out for at least one day to protest Walker's cut to educational funding and his plan to curtail collective bargaining. Their union, Madison Teachers Inc., proved to be one of the best-organized groups of the spring events. Meanwhile, members of the UW faculty also stepped forward. One group lost no time in putting up a Facebook page, UW–Madison Faculty Organizing for Change, which posted information about upcoming events designed to respond to the governor's proposed legislation, especially those aspects dealing with collective bargaining, health insurance, and pensions. Outside Madison, UW faculty members issued their own challenge to Walker by voting to unionize. While the Madison faculty demurred, the faculties at other campuses in the UW System had earlier joined the Association of University of Wisconsin Professionals, a lobbying group affiliated with the American Federation of Teachers (AFT); after Walker introduced the budget repair bill, they voted overwhelmingly to form bargaining units. By the end of March, faculty and academic staff members at the University of Wisconsin's Stout, LaCrosse, and River Falls campuses had joined the Eau Claire campus in establishing AFT–Wisconsin unions. UW–Green Bay and UW–Superior followed later in the spring. In the face of provisions in the budget repair bill that would effectively dismantle state unions, collective bargaining looked better and better as a means of protecting the university system.

Others found their own voices. Faculty members at the University of Wisconsin–Whitewater, still not unionized in March, nonetheless composed a collective letter to Walker underscoring the harm his budget reductions would do to them as a faculty and, especially, to students at all levels. Heading into an unseasonably cold weekend in late March, a small group of UW–Whitewater professors walked forty-three miles from their campus to the capitol to hand-deliver their missive. Meanwhile, state employees and large numbers of UW faculty across the system pledged solidarity with other state workers, the elementary and high school teachers, corrections officers, and nurses who swelled the ranks of protesters. What did these nonacademics have in common, other than being threatened by Walker's budget bill? The majority were graduates of one branch or another of the University of Wisconsin. Faculty members spoke at the capitol rallies and smaller simultaneous protests from Green Bay to River Falls and LaCrosse to Milwaukee, while others wrote op-ed pieces for national and local newspapers, and still others appeared on radio and television talk shows.

The importance of the University of Wisconsin System in service to the state was further reflected in the educational backgrounds of the state legislators themselves. All but six of the nineteen Republicans and fourteen Democrats in the state senate had attended the UW, the overwhelming majority a branch campus outside Madison. In the state assembly, the principal adversaries, the Republican majority leader and the Democratic minority leader, were likewise holders of UW degrees. In contrast, the governor himself lacked a college diploma, having dropped out of Marquette University. Some protesters picked up quickly and a bit meanly on this theme. Teachers' signs at the rallies read: "Anyone can be governor, while it takes a college education to do my job."

The Wisconsin state legislature was not unique in having its educational roots in the state's university system. Compared with their counterparts in other states, though, state legislators were more likely to have bachelor's degrees and far more likely to have earned them in the state's public colleges and universities. This affinity, however, did not necessarily ensure loyalty to Wisconsin's institutions of higher learning or even promote respect for educators at any level. Nevertheless, one of Walker's first major defeats was his proposal, allegedly hatched in secret with the UW–Madison chancellor, Biddy Martin, to break the flagship campus off from the rest of the system, thereby jeopardizing the academic standing and financial solvency of the campuses outside Madison. Protesters and the board of regents alike prepared to save the UW System, put the governor's plan into limbo, and give Chancellor Martin good reason to resign and flee to the calmer administrative waters of Amherst College, where he became the nineteenth president in August 2011.

THE TAA LEADS THE WAY

A leader in organizing the protests against Governor Walker was the UW–Madison Teaching Assistants' Association (TAA), the first successful union of graduate student teaching assistants anywhere. The TAA had emerged in the mid-1960s amid antiwar protests and student strikes over the university's complicity in Vietnam, but also over curricular and parietal issues. After the state legislature proposed a bill eliminating out-of-state tuition remission for graduate assistants, the then-small TAA voted to strike if necessary. The legislature withdrew its bill, but the wheels of collective bargaining had been set into motion. Graduate students successfully voted for bargaining rights in 1969. When the UW administration stalled, the TAA called a strike. Just four weeks later, with the help of local Teamsters who refused to cross picket lines, in early 1970 the students won most of their demands, including guaranteed support for three to four years, grievance procedures, workload limitations (such as number of students and class size), and health insurance. It was a revolution of sorts for campus life, and not only in Madison or across Wisconsin.

During the decades that followed, the TAA provided a steady presence on campus and, increasingly, far beyond. In 1974 the TAA affiliated with the AFT and added its badly needed energy, first to the local labor council and then to the flagging state labor movement. David Newby, first elected as a graduate student to the leadership of the TAA, rose in 1982 to the presidency of the Madison Central Labor Council and by 1993 to the presidency of the Wisconsin AFL-CIO, a position he held until his retirement in 2010. Repeatedly threatened by university takebacks, the TAA built solid support among the ever-shifting base of graduate students, and by 2011 represented 3,000 teaching assistants. Current TAA members immediately grasped the significance of the budget repair bill's provisions to abrogate state employees' union contracts, including the curtailment of automatic deduction of union dues from paychecks (known as the checkoff) and the requirement to recertify recognition each year.

Extremely well-organized TAA members took some of the first steps to foster the wider protest movement. Because of the fluidity of TAA membership, union activists had carefully developed over the years what one historian-activist described as a "unique internal political culture" marked by "a conscious, thoughtfully articulated, sometimes contested collective memory." This political culture, which one of its websites defines explicitly as the promotion of "progressive values in the Wisconsin tradition," became better known within weeks of Walker's inauguration.

The TAA leadership acted on the Wisconsin Idea. On the stormy night of Walker's inauguration speech on January 3, TAA members and others gathered in the UW Memorial Union Rathskeller to watch the televised event. They listened as the state's forty-fifth governor repeated his campaign pledge to "work with our legislative part-ners—in both political parties—to pass a series of bold reforms that will send a clear message: 'Wisconsin is open for business.'" The TAA was not the first group to respond. That morning, at the governor's inaugural prayer breakfast, a group of approximately 700 protesters, many from Milwaukee, gathered outside. Many carried signs with a message that would become familiar in the next several months: "The Rich Get Richer, Workers Get Sacked." TAA members, along with the the Student Labor Action Coalition, an organization mainly of under-graduates, also began to contemplate their future roles and met with members of the Labor and Working Class Studies Project (a collabora-tive campus-labor-community initiative), the UW School for Workers, and various professors and union leaders.

On February 12, just before the governor's introduction of the budget repair bill, they began to plan a protest action. A tense meeting followed two days later. In a packed campus lecture hall, TAA leaders declared that Wisconsin had reached a turning point in its history and urged those present to put aside their other work for as long as the struggle would take. Their collective house, for the present, was the state capitol itself.

Issuing a bulletin that called upon members to "stand up, fight back!" the TAA helped to rally more than a thousand activists from the UW community in the capitol rotunda, where they delivered val-entines to Walker that professed their love of UW and demanded a halt to budget cuts.

The TAA then helped organize the famous occupation that would last weeks. The legislature's Joint Financial Committee opened hearings on the budget repair bill, and TAA recruited hundreds upon hundreds of individuals to speak in the two-minute segments allotted. When the hearings continued into the night, the TAA advised members to preserve their places on the list and stay at the capitol. Meanwhile, the American Federation of State, County and Municipal Employees (AFSCME) began to sponsor buses from cities outside Madison and urged its members to ride to the capitol to, as one popular chant specified, "kill the bill."

Tens of thousands of other Wisconsin residents joined the protest in the capitol, including UW undergraduates and professors and staff members, but also firefighters, corrections officers, private-sector unionists, members of faith communities, and a hardy crew of Madison-style, graying-but-activist retirees. Given such numbers and such diversity, the message was clear: these protesters were not leaving, and the political cost of pushing them out by force would be great.

The TAA breathed new life into the Wisconsin Idea, strengthening the link between the university and the citizenry in a dramatic fashion. Members played a decisive role in keeping the crowd peaceful and orderly—and thus safe and comfortable for the disabled, elderly, and parents with babies in their arms. TAA members coordinated the staffing of the food table, which depended on volunteers to distribute tons of donated food—especially pizza—and coffee. TAA members also formed cleaning brigades that swept the building several times daily and even sought to ensure that only painters' tape was used to put up protest signs, thereby protecting the marble of the capitol walls. A "war room" set up in the capitol, meanwhile, provided the strategy center where TAA'ers decided upon immediate tasks, posted minute-by-minute updates on Twitter, wrote press releases, set up actions, and acted as a hub that made the long-term occupation of the capitol viable. Among its greatest, most visible and long-lasting services was a Facebook page, Defend Wisconsin. Here the TAA posted major news stories about GOP legislative plans and citizens' pushback. Especially important was the calendar of events, an invaluable source, updated frequently throughout the day, for anyone interested in participating in rallies, recalls, or special events such as Walkerville, the tent city that ringed the Wisconsin Capitol during June 2011 and was modeled on the Hoovervilles of the Great Depression.

As the days wore on, TAA activists did much to make it possible, in a multitude of small ways, for protesters to maintain their continual, always peaceful, presence. Quiet hours began at 10 p.m., air mattresses were provided for some people, and a lending library was established for insomniacs. The delivery of food and water continued and now included evening meals for AFSCME members who helped to maintain the two-week vigil. During the day, when speeches, drumming, and chanting moved to the higher decibels, TAA members even supplied a box of earplugs, which was especially important for young children. And to give parents with children a respite from the noise and crowds in the rotunda, the TAA maintained a quiet room in the capitol basement. The medic station even included a massage chair, and the shelves of the women's bathrooms were lined with feminine hygiene products, diapers, and wipes. Hand sanitizers were scattered throughout the building, and recycling was mandatory.

The TAA and AFSCME members won the respect of the capitol police. Charged by Walker in late February with removing the protesters, the capitol police chief refused to do so, claiming that the occupation was so peaceful and orderly that forceful intervention was both unnecessary and potentially injurious to both protesters and police. Chief Charles Tubb went so far as to commend the behavior and cooperation of the protesters. By this time dozens of members of the Wisconsin Police Union, a surprisingly friendly presence, had joined the overnight protesters in the capitol occupation.

By March 3, when protesters finally left the capitol, it was clear that the "first act of the drama" (as returned Democratic senators named it at a March 12 rally) was now over. By late June, when the governor signed the law that sealed the budget for the next two years, the second act, which brought out decreasing numbers of protesters, had also ended. Still, as signs insisted, "Still Our Wisconsin," and perhaps third, and other acts remained to be played out, with so many twists and turns of events that no certain outcome was likely to be determined anytime soon.

Yet something irrevocable had happened, certainly in Wisconsin, and perhaps with implications far beyond. In 1912 Charles McCarthy, the state's reference librarian, published a book documenting the Wisconsin Idea and describing in considerable detail the pathbreaking legislation that served as a beacon for Progressives nationwide. The legislative session of 1911, he wrote, was "perhaps the most remarkable session ever held in any state, and not only in the humanitarian spirit of the laws but also in the daring manner in which great questions were handled." A century later the Wisconsin GOP effected equally daring changes in the laws governing the state and likewise sought to make Wisconsin the model, this time in the form of a marriage of government and business rather than the expression of popular democracy. The contrast between the Wisconsin Idea and Walker's vision could not be sharper.

Still, the Wisconsin Idea shone brightly in the hearts of the protesters, who ended their spring initiative by claiming to have constituted a genuine people's movement. The traditions of the Progressive era, amazingly alive in the twenty-first century, had been refurbished in ways that made standard politicians' (or historians') references to the Founders or even the Second World War seem abstract. Nor was this a mystery. Progressives had responded to conditions and behavior, economic and political, that now seem eerily familiar, more so than anyone could have guessed only a few years ago.

Factories have all but disappeared, taking private-sector union memberships with them. The farmers who once rallied to Bob La Follette are now relatively few. But the workforce of the new century—educators and others in the social services sector, along with the wider public—has boldly stepped forward to fill the breach.

FURTHER READING

Czitrom, Daniel, "Reeling in the Years," *Academe* 96, no. 1, January–February 2010, 34–36.

Maxwell, Robert S., *La Follette and the Rise of the Progressives in Wisconsin,* Madison: State Historical Society of Wisconsin, 1956.

McCarthy, Charles, *The Wisconsin Idea*, New York: Macmillan, 1912.

Thelen, David P., *Robert M. La Follette and the Insurgent Spirit*, Boston: Little, Brown, 1976.

3 FROSTBITE AND FREEDOM: THE BATTLE OF MADISON

By Tom Morello

I met my friends at a local townie bar across the street. At this bar were two big, burly, drunken Packer fans. The kind of fellas I might normally avoid if I ran into them on tour, but things are different here in Madison. These big, teddy bear Packer fans were even more militant in support of the union and of the protests than the kids in the capitol. These guys led the entire bar in blaring pro-union chants (and anti–Governor Walker slurs), and they may have even bought a round of shots or two for some of the skinny musicians in the corner.

After a few spirited hours, I was certain: these people in Wisconsin are not going to give up, they are not going to give in, and if there is any justice in this world, these good people will defeat Governor Walker's awful antiunion bill. This right-wing governor tried to take advantage of a recession brought on by Wall Street malfeasance to try to ram through legislation that would roll back decades of social progress. But he and his corporate shot callers miscalculated by taking on *these* people. We didn't ask for this fight; Governor Walker tapped us on the shoulder and said, "Let's fight." Okay, dude, it's on. And now we're going to knock your legislative teeth out.

The next morning, we met with union representatives and each musician was paired with a local Wisconsin worker for side-by-side interviews by reporters, because it was important for all of us to keep the emphasis on the workers involved in this struggle on a daily basis. I spent the next few hours talking to reporters with Natalie Parker, a nurse and member of the Service Employees International Union (SEIU) Local 1199, and her young daughter. I learned from them that this was not a fight about fixing a broken state budget, as the governor claimed. The unions had already conceded every single economic issue at hand. The only issue that they refused concede, that they should never concede, was the right to bargain collectively—the right to be in a union and the right to stand together. This is especially crucial in the area of education. The five states that outlaw collective bargaining (South Carolina, North Carolina, Georgia, Texas, and Virginia) are the five states with the lowest SAT/ACT scores in the country. Where does Wisconsin, with its strong teachers' union, rank? Second.

At noon we were off to Capitol Square to finally play some music. Madison's mayor estimated that more than half a million people had marched there over ten days without a single arrest. So, despite the frigid temperatures and a whipping, icy wind, the crowd was huge, peaceful, and pumped. First up was Ike Reilly, whose homespun tales and improvised lyrics about the struggle struck a chord with the crowd of thousands. Next up was the band Street Dogs, who played an inspired cover of Billy Bragg's "There Is Power in a Union" and an original called "Up the Union" that had the crowd roaring. Wayne Kramer then rocked a number of great tunes as we awaited the arrival of the rest of the day's labor delegation. Poor Wayne's luggage had not made the trip to Madison, so he was out there fighting the good fight in a thin coat as his fingers turned frostbite blue. Tim from Rise Against somehow played dexterous versions of Neil Young's "Ohio" and Credence Clearwater's "Who'll Stop the Rain?" while his angelic punk-rock voice echoed through the streets.

Next up was yours truly, The Nightwatchman. I opened my set with "Union Song," which I wrote for days like this. ("Now dirty scabs will cross the line/While others stand aside and look/But ain't nobody never got nothin'/That didn't raise their voice and push!") By the end of "Union Song," I had no feeling in my fingers, and it felt like I had frozen crab claws at the ends of my arms. I actually dropped my guitar pick at one point and didn't even realize it because I couldn't feel my claws. For the finale all the musicians came on stage for a version of Woody Guthrie's "This Land Is Your Land." We reinserted the radical verses that were censored when you learned this people's jam in the third grade, such as: "In the squares of the city/In the shadow of the steeple/Near the relief office/I see my people/Some are grumblin'/And all are wonderin'/If this land's still made for you and me." The crowd pogo-ed all around the capitol, and with the spirit of solidarity in the air, it was clear to me that if we stuck together, we were going to win this fight.

Next, the whole gang went into the capitol, which was thunderous with a wild drum circle punctuating a speech given by the president of the United Steelworkers, who vowed to keep steelworkers in the capitol 24/7 to defend the protesters from eviction. He dared Governor Walker to come debate this issue face to face. The chants and drums were deafening. It really felt like the eye of a hurricane, the dawn of a thrilling new movement. The scene made me think of the famous Gandhi quote: "First they ignore you, then they ridicule you, then they fight you, then you win."

I was standing down the hallway from the speeches, wanting to get a closer look, when all of a sudden several union reps started yelling, "Clear a path for The Nightwatchman! Clear a path for The Nightwatchman!" Well, The Nightwatchman and his crab claws just wanted to warm up and watch the festivities, but then someone shoved a bullhorn in my face and stood me on top of a rickety chair, and I was pressed into delivering an impromptu speech. I related our experiences so far and said what an inspiration the people of Wisconsin were to me and to all those who support workers' rights around this country. I told them that I've been a proud union man for twenty-two years, as part of Musicians' Local 47 in Los Angeles, and a red card–carrying member of the Industrial Workers of the World, and that for me this fight was personal, because my mom, Mary Morello, was a public high school teacher for almost three decades in Libertyville, Illinois. And while we never had much money, we always had enough food on the table, and we had clothes on our backs, because my mom was a union teacher. And if Governor Walker was going to attack the rights of people like my mom, then The Nightwatchman was coming for his ass.

Part 2 THE RIGHT-WING ASSAULT

4 THE SALE OF WISCONSIN

By Mary Bottari

In the 2010 elections Republicans emerged with seven more governors. They also won control of twenty-six state legislatures, up from fourteen. In many trifecta states, where a new Republican majority won control of both houses and the governorship, an odd thing happened. A steady stream of almost identical bills—bills to defund unions and make it harder for democratic constituencies to vote, bills to privatize schools and public assets, bills to enshrine corporate tax loopholes while crippling the government's ability to raise revenue—were introduced and passed. Almost identical sets of corporations benefited from these measures.

It is almost as if a pipeline in the basement of these state capitols ruptured simultaneously and a flood of special interest legislation poured out. The blowout preventer, the tradition of sharing political power, had been disabled. The source of the contamination? The American Legislative Exchange Council (ALEC).

Decades ago, ALEC targeted Wisconsin as a test case for its agenda. Tommy Thompson, who served as a state legislator from 1966 to 1987 and then as governor for a record fourteen years, was an early ALEC member and supporter. "Myself, I always loved going to these meetings because I always found new ideas. Then I'd take them back to Wisconsin, disguise them a little bit, and declare that it's mine," he told an ALEC conference in 2002.

It is now apparent that Thomson was the enthusiastic front man for a slew of ALEC bills, most famously, "Welfare to Work" and "School Choice." In 1990 Milwaukee's school voucher program for children of low-income families was the first in the nation, the camel's nose under the tent for a long-term agenda whose ultimate goal is the privatization of public schools. Wisconsin's new governor, Scott Walker, decided to follow in Thompson's footsteps, pushing a half-dozen ALEC bills through the legislature during his first weeks and months in office yet remaining silent about the roots of these so-called public policy innovations.

CRAFTING THE "POLITICALLY INEVITABLE"

ALEC is not a lobby, nor is it a front group, but something much more powerful than that. Behind closed doors, corporations hand legislators the law changes that directly benefit their bottom line. The corporations fund 98 percent of ALEC's operations directly through hefty membership dues and indirectly through corporate foundations, like the Charles G. Koch Foundation. Corporate officers sit on ALEC's task forces and work with legislators to draft model bills, which are kept secret from the public. They wine and dine legislators at swank US resort hotels, with child care provided, fund-raisers and other perks prearranged. In turn, participating legislators, overwhelmingly conservative Republicans, bring the bills home and introduce them into statehouses across the land as their own brilliant ideas and important public policy innovations.

ALEC's agenda is not modest. In her groundbreaking book *Shock Doctrine*, Naomi Klein coined the term "disaster capitalism" to refer to the rapid-fire corporate reengineering of societies still reeling from shock. The master of disaster? The free-market guru and University of Chicago economist Milton Friedman, who famously said: "Only a crisis—actual or perceived—produces real changes. When the crisis occurs, the actions that are taken depend on the ideas that are lying around. That, I believe, is our basic function: to develop alternatives to existing policies to keep them alive and available until the politically impossible becomes politically inevitable."

The Wall Street financial crisis, caused by years of deregulation and lack of government oversight, cost Americans $14 trillion in lost wealth and eight million lost jobs. The jobs crisis tanked federal and state tax receipts, creating predictable budget shortfalls. Rather than being chastened for its starring role in the catastrophe, the GOP moved into high gear with its spin machine, blaming budget shortfalls on reckless overspending and public employees who were living high on the hog.

ALEC moved swiftly to capitalize on the crisis. In 2008, Indiana governor Mitch Daniels crowed to an ALEC State and Nation Policy Summit, "This is a terrific time to shrink government," and the ALEC shock troops swung into high gear.

New GOP governors across the nation reached for the "ideas ... lying around" in the corporate library called ALEC. In Indiana, Ohio, Michigan, Maine, New Jersey, and Florida, bill after bill was introduced. Bills, that is, that would, among other things, wipe out a state's ability to raise revenue; eviscerate public services; financially destroy Democratic supporters, such as trial lawyers and unions; make it harder for key Democratic constituencies to vote; lock up large numbers of immigrants; and prevent the implementation of the federal health-care reform bill.

THE WISCONSIN MEN FROM ALEC

Three men have dominated the agenda of radical transformation in the State of Wisconsin. All three have long been ALEC members and active participants: Governor Scott Walker, Senate Majority Leader Scott Fitzgerald, and Assembly Speaker Jeff Fitzgerald.

Walker was an active member of ALEC as a state legislator, from 1993 to 2002, even listing his ALEC membership in his *Wisconsin Blue Book* profile. As a young legislator in the 1990s, he worked with then-governor Tommy Thompson in a successful effort to pass ALEC's "Truth in Sentencing" bill. The law benefited mainly the Corrections Corporation of America (CCA), which for many years housed overflow Wisconsin inmates out of state. When the bill was passed, CCA was the corporate cochair of ALEC's Criminal Justice Task Force. But not in a public way.

The modus operandi had been set in place. The former Wisconsin corrections administrator, Walter Dickey, who paid close attention to the debate about truth in sentencing in Madison, claimed: "There was never any mention [by proponents] that ALEC or anybody else had any involvement" in crafting the bill. The authors of the bill, their goals, and their interests were never disclosed to the public. Instead, their agenda was presented as in the best interests of the Wisconsin criminal justice system and taxpayers. In 2011 Walker drew on his experiences as a loyal ALEC foot soldier and introduced many ALEC bills "by request of the Governor."

The Republican wave that gave Scott Walker the governorship also gave the GOP control of both houses. Scott Fitzgerald became the state senate majority leader; Jeff Fitzgerald became the speaker of the state assembly. The Fitzgerald brothers, born in Chicago, had moved to Dodge County, Wisconsin, as students. In recent years they had played a critical role in moving the state GOP further to the right and enthusiastically embraced their new role as Walker's chief lieutenants.

After running on a platform of jobs and economic development, Scott Fitzgerald started opening up about his big plans for the state shortly after the 2010 election: "Listen, we have new majorities; if you talk to the members of the House of the Representatives and the way they view the world right now, the more feathers you ruffle right now, the stronger you are going to be politically. I don't ever remember an environment where that existed before. It was always go along, get along. A little on the edges, yeah, we would take a few shots here and there at some political enemies, but in the end we all just wanted to be on the same page. That just doesn't exist right now. I've never seen that before; it gives us a lot of leeway and a lot of chain to make some significant changes."

Walker announced to the *Milwaukee Journal Sentinel* that his first effort would be a "Voter ID" bill; it would disenfranchise traditional Democratic constituencies, like the poor, black, and elderly, who are less likely to have official photo identification. ALEC had produced model voter ID legislation in the summer of 2009, less than a year after Barack Obama had been elected president.

The second strike? Only reporters paying close attention might have noticed a December 2010 interview in which Fitzgerald was asked about making Wisconsin a "right to work" state, that is, a hostile work environment for private-sector unions. "I just attended an American Legislative Exchange Council and I was surprised about how much momentum there was in and around that discussion, nothing like I have seen before," said Fitzgerald enthusiastically.

This was the first, but hardly the last, time the name of ALEC would surface in the lexicon of Wisconsin's new state order, dubbed "Fitzwalkerstan" by the Democratic legislator Marc Pocan. Scott Fitzgerald had served as ALEC's Wisconsin state chairman for many years. Economic interest statements filed with the state show that in 2010 and 2011, state senator Scott Fitzgerald received almost

$3,000 from ALEC to attend its conferences. In 2011 state representative Jeff Fitzgerald received $1,329. Thus it is hardly a surprise that Republican legislators brought a huge variety of ALEC's model bills home to Wisconsin.

Together with other ALEC members, such as Robin Vos, chair of the powerful Joint Finance Committee (and ALEC state chair for Wisconsin), and state senator Leah Vukmir, chair of Wisconsin's Heath Committee (she also chairs ALEC's Health and Human Service Task Force), the Fitzgerald brothers rushed dozens of ALEC specials through the legislature and onto the governor's desk. Why the hurry? The August 2011 recall elections for nine state senators that might hand control of the state senate to Democrats were not far away.

ALEC BILLS INTRODUCED IN THE WISCONSIN LEGISLATURE

DEFUNDING UNIONS AND ATTACKING COLLECTIVE BARGAINING

Wisconsin governor Scott Walker took a cue from the ALEC corporate wish list and sent to the legislature in February 2011 a radical bill designed to cripple public employee unions. Several other Republican governors considered similar legislation, but few could claim to be moving against history: Wisconsin was one of the first states to grant public workers the right to bargain over wages and conditions.

No ALEC bill precisely mirrors Walker's proposal, but the Wisconsin bill does comport with ALEC's sweeping antiunion agenda, which includes decades of support for "right to work" and "paycheck protection" legislation and other measures to disempower and defund unions. On collective bargaining, ALEC's "Public Employees Freedom Act" declares that "an employee should be able to contract on their own terms," and "mandatory collective bargaining laws violate this freedom." This ALEC bill and the organization's "Public Employer Payroll Deduction Act" prohibit automatic payroll deductions for union dues, a key aspect of Walker's bill.

These bills were designed to cripple the key financial supporter of Democratic candidates just in time for the 2012 presidential election. Similarly, ALEC's slew of "tort reform" measures was designed to harm trial lawyers, another traditional Democratic constituency. A package of ALEC tort reform bills that make it harder for injured Americans to sue was one of the first bills introduced and passed in 2011.

Where is the bottom in ALEC's race to the bottom? "The Living Wage Mandate Preemptions Act" would repeal any local living wage ordinance, like the ones in Madison and Milwaukee, and prohibit a political subdivision from enacting such a measure in the future. The ALEC "Prevailing Wage Repeal Act" would get rid of all state laws that guarantee workers employed under public works contracts are paid the wage that prevails in their industry. The ALEC "Starting Minimum Wage Repeal Act" would preempt the ability of states and localities to pay a minimum wage higher than the federal level. Twenty-two states do this, but ALEC objects to the policy as an "unfunded mandate." Another ALEC bill promotes prison industries, where minimum wage laws do not apply. ALEC also supports a radical free-trade agenda that pits US workers against foreign workers making a fraction of their wage and facilitates the offshoring of US jobs. From China Free Trade in 2000 to Korea Free Trade today, ALEC has supported the shipping of jobs overseas.

TRIMMING AWAY VOTER RIGHTS AND PUBLIC FINANCING

If Walker's bill curtailing many of the rights to collective bargaining for public workers resulted in weakening the financial base of Democratic candidates, companion legislation was aimed even more precisely at that target.

On May 19, 2011, Wisconsin passed a "Voter ID" law introduced by Republican state representative Jeff Stone and state senator Joe Leibham. Stone, an ALEC member, received ALEC travel reimbursements in 2009. The legislation would allow citizens to present certain narrow types of identification, including a driver's license and state-issued ID cards, in order to vote. According to a UW–Milwaukee study, about 177,000 Wisconsinites aged sixty-five and older do not have any state-issued identification. Statewide, only 45 percent of African American men and 51 percent of African American women have a valid driver's license. Not every county has an office of the Wisconsin Department of Motor Vehicles, which keeps irregular hours. This creates significant barriers to obtaining photo IDs.

The bill makes voting especially burdensome for college students, a group that overwhelmingly supported Obama in 2008. Student IDs have to be issued by an accredited public or private college, include the student's signature, and have a two-year expiration date. IDs for the

182,000 students in the University of Wisconsin System and 300,000 enrolled in state technical colleges currently do not meet these requirements.

Voter ID legislation is ostensibly designed to prevent voter fraud. After a statewide investigation in 2008, the Wisconsin attorney general, a Republican, found no evidence of voter fraud. The bill is an effort "to prevent Democratic groupings from turning out, and everybody knows it," said Jay Heck of Wisconsin Common Cause. When the bill passed, Walker tweeted, "Glad that Photo ID bill passed. I authored that bill 10 years ago!"—back when he was an active ALEC member. The Wisconsin bill is a more detailed version of the ALEC "Voter ID Act" of 2009.

To pay for the Voter ID law the Wisconsin Joint Finance Committee appropriated money that had been set aside for the public financing of campaigns. The money taken from the public financing system—$1.8 million—was insufficient to underwrite the costs of the measure, which was expected to cost $6 million to implement in its first two years. However, the move would end a thirty-four-year tradition of public financing for elections in Wisconsin. All public financing for state political races would end.

GIVING TAX BREAKS TO BIG TOBACCO

The legislation targeting collective bargaining and voting rights attracted the most attention and opposition, but even more ALEC bills succeeded by stealth.

A series of ALEC bills, stuffed into the 2011 Wisconsin state budget, received little scrutiny; among them were the reinstatement of the "Las Vegas Loophole," which allows firms to hide income acquired out of state; lower taxes on capital gains; new provisions allowing bounty hunters into the state for the first time; and even a measure banning mandatory recycling.

On May 31, 2011, Republican state senators Alberta Darling and Luther Olsen rolled a motion in the Wisconsin budget bill that would have given a big tax break to a Big Tobacco company. The Wisconsin Joint Finance Committee voted to convert the tax on moist tobacco products from a price-based tax to a weight-based tax. Moist tobacco products like Skol, Copenhagen, and a new product line called Snus—which is increasingly popular with preadolescent and adolescent boys—would have benefited from this tax break. These tax changes would have lowered the price of the smokeless products that target young people with packaging and candy flavors like cherry, apple, and grape, according to Emily Rohloff, a spokeswoman for a statewide coalition of health groups. The committee also cut funds for the Tobacco Prevention and Control program by 22 percent.

Darling, who used her campaign account to fly to ALEC meetings, also slipped into the budget bill a measure identical to ALEC's "Resolution on the Enhancement of Economic Neutrality, Commercial Efficiency and Fairness in the Taxation of Moist Smokeless Tobacco Products" that specifically promoted this tax break. ALEC, serving as a front for tobacco interests, sent a letter to Scott Walker in support of the measure, which passed as part of the budget bill. However, after more than a dozen public health groups objected to this measure, it proved so extreme and politically embarrassing that the governor vetoed it.

KNEECAPPING SMALL BREWERIES

Darling also rolled a measure into the state budget bill that threatened the welfare of one of the state's most beloved and successful products: craft beer. This measure effectively bars small brewers from starting a wholesale company. Current breweries lost their wholesale and retail licenses, and the law prohibits breweries from owning a restaurant separate from the brewery and selling their products through it. The bill affects such popular brands as Oso, Hinterland, Milwaukee Ale House, Great Dane, and Capital Brewing. The law largely benefits one firm, the Miller-Coors behemoth.

The measure was backed by the Wisconsin Beer Distributors Association, which is the local chapter of the National Beer Wholesalers Association (NBWA). NBWA sits on the ALEC corporate Private Enterprise Board, which has a powerful governing role in the organization. According to MapLight.org, a nonprofit, nonpartisan research organization, liquor wholesalers were big supporters of the Fitzgerald brothers, contributing $18,417 to Scott Fitzgerald and $16,353 to Jeff Fitzgerald in recent years. Liquor wholesalers also gave Darling $5,200. Miller-Coors alone contributed $28,000 to Scott Walker's gubernatorial race. Despite considerable opposition and continuing criticism, even from members of his own party, Walker refused to veto this legislation.

INCOME PROTECTION FOR ROAD BUILDERS

On May 19, 2011, the Wisconsin legislature approved Senate Joint Resolution 23, which was introduced by Republican state senator Randy Hopper. By this action, the legislature voted to seek approval from the electorate for a constitutional amendment that would restrict to road building and repairs the expenditure of funds generated by gas taxes and vehicle registration and fees. This measure would prevent the money from being used for any other important state priorities and would favor fossil-fuel-powered vehicles on highways over all other modes of transportation. The measure has been adopted in more than twenty states and is considered to be a dangerous weapon against a smart and diverse transportation policy. Before the constitution can be amended, Wisconsin law requires that the legislature vote once more to send the amendment to voters, and that voters approve it in a statewide referendum.

During his eight years in office, Democratic governor Jim Doyle borrowed $1.3 billion from the transportation fund to pay for schools. Lawmakers from both parties signed off on many of those transfers. In the debate about the proposed constitutional amendment, Democratic state senator Fred Risser commented: "I am not sure why we think roads are more important than schools."

The bill is based on an ALEC bill of the same name: "Constitutional Amendment Restricting the Use of Vehicle Fees and Taxes for Highway Purposes." The measure came on top of Walker's controversial decision to reject $800 million in federal funds to build a high-speed rail connection between Madison and Milwaukee. Both measures would directly benefit one of Walker's biggest campaign contributors, the road-building lobby. According to the Wisconsin Democracy Campaign, a nonpartisan clean government group, the road builders gave Walker $156,907 for his gubernatorial race. According to Maplight.org, Hopper received $11,350 from contributors linked to road construction interest groups.

CARING FOR THE INSURANCE INDUSTRY

A major agenda item for ALEC for many decades has been to protect the health insurance industry from regulations that control costs, provide important services, and aid consumers. ALEC has also been a leading proponent of the privatization of Medicare and Medicaid, fielding multiple bills to turn these programs into voucher plans that allow the insurance industry to siphon off millions in fees.

In an interview with Madison's *Capital Times*, Scott Fitzgerald talked openly about ALEC's health-care agenda. Fitzgerald told the paper that in December 2010, he and twenty to thirty other Wisconsin GOP lawmakers attended ALEC's national meeting in Washington, DC, where a key topic was federal health-care reform. ALEC's "State Legislators' Guide to Repealing Obamacare" was handed out at this meeting, and a list of related model legislation was discussed. "A good example of that is a bill Joe Leibham is working on right now," Fitzgerald told the paper.

Leibham and Vos introduced the Health Care Freedom Amendment in March 2011. The bill would send yet another constitutional amendment to voters, this time to change the Wisconsin Constitution to prohibit the government from forcing anyone to participate in any public or private health-care or insurance program. The bill is modeled on an ALEC bill of the same name and is a direct attack on the Patient Protection and Affordable Health Care Act passed by Congress in 2010. The proposed amendment came on top of national GOP efforts to block implementation of the federal legislation by challenging it in court in many states. According to ALEC, in 2010 the Health Care Freedom Amendment was introduced in forty-two states. Six states (Virginia, Idaho, Arizona, Georgia, Louisiana, and Missouri) passed it statutorily, and two states (Arizona and Oklahoma) passed it as a constitutional amendment. But twenty-five states rejected the measure as blatantly unconstitutional.

"TELL US ABOUT ALEC"

William Cronon, a professor of history, geography, and environmental studies at the University of Wisconsin–Madison, is not merely a public employee. He is also the prize-winning author of numerous groundbreaking books and the recently elected president of the American Historical Association. During the opening weeks of Walker's administration, Cronon became interested in the historical roots of the GOP agenda. On his blog "Scholar as Citizen," he wrote about his investigations, giving students and interested parties some tips on how to investigative the shadowy groups that he thought might be behind the onslaught of legislation.

Cronon rightly focused on ALEC, writing:

> The most important group, I'm pretty sure, is the American Legislative Exchange Council (ALEC), which was founded in 1973 by Henry Hyde, Lou Barnett, and (surprise, surprise) Paul Weyrich. Its goal for the past forty years has been to draft "model bills" that conservative legislators can introduce in the 50 states.

Even Cronon was surprised by the reaction to his intervention. Because Cronon is a respected historian and a self-described political centrist, his piece got around quite a bit. His blog received more than a half million hits. Handmade signs quickly popped up at the Wisconsin Capitol such as "Tell Me about ALEC."

To Cronon's further astonishment, the pushback was immediate. Like avenging furies, the Wisconsin GOP filed an open records request demanding all of Cronon's university emails referencing Scott Walker, collective bargaining, and a long list of Republican legislators, fruitlessly attempting to prove that Cronon was involved in partisan political activities. This occurred even before Cronon wrote a compelling op-ed piece for the *New York Times* in which he discussed Wisconsin's radical break from its long tradition of clean government and moderation. The GOP'S overreaction signaled that something important was going on in Wisconsin, something Republicans did not want to discuss publicly.

FURTHER READING

"ALEC Exposed," website (alecexposed.org) of the Center for Media and Democracy, a nonprofit investigative reporting group that inventories all ALEC's model bills.

The Nation, August 18, 2011, includes a special section, "ALEC Exposed."

5 THE WAR ON SCHOOLS

By Ruth Conniff

The public outpouring was incredible. People flooded into the capitol in Madison, Wisconsin, from the urban neighborhoods of Milwaukee and tiny towns in the northern and western corners of the state. They came to oppose Republican plans that would wipe out rural school districts, drain resources from city schools, and dismantle an entire statewide system of public education. They packed a hearing room and two overflow rooms, and waited all day to speak. Hour after hour, teachers, parents, and citizens gave impassioned, often tearful, testimony. Jon Sheller, a former member of the Montello school board, and his daughter, social studies teacher Yedda Ligocki, talked about their little town, with 750 schoolchildren. "As in most small school districts," Sheller said, the school "is the heart of the community." "The athletics, the musicals, other school activities are the life of Montello," Ligocki added. Governor Scott Walker's unprecedented $900 million cut to school funding, coupled with a scheme to create a state-run system of charter schools, will kill off both the school and the town, they said.

The new education legislation would siphon off money that used to go public schools like Montello's and redirect it to charter schools run, if the governor had his way, by a state board of political appointees. "There will be no turning back," Sheller said. "Small schools and their communities will wither and die—and for what? A political maneuver to allow privatization of public education at the expense of Wisconsin's history as a leader in student achievement. This is giving away our future."

Wisconsin is on the leading edge of a national assault on public education. Walker made a big name for himself with his explosive move to bust public employee unions and take away teachers' bargaining rights. Now comes the next phase. "We've been hearing about this for years now," said Democratic state representative Sondy Pope-Roberts. "I see Wisconsin as the first domino in a line. As this falls, I see other states hoping to achieve our 'success' ... by crushing unions and taking public schools private."

Wisconsin has long had a strong public school system. Even as Walker was declaring Wisconsin "open for business," describing his budget cuts and more than $500 million in new tax breaks for corporations as part of a plan to attract business to Wisconsin, Forward Wisconsin, a nonprofit corporation established by the state to market Wisconsin's assets to corporate executives, was touting high-quality schools as one of the state's major selling points.

Among the "statistics and facts about Wisconsin's great schools" the group promotes on its website:

- Wisconsin ranks first in the nation in the percentage of teachers who meet the federal standard of "highly qualified" under the revised Elementary and Secondary Education Act (No Child Left Behind).
- Wisconsin is a national leader in public high-school graduation rates, ranking first or second among the states from 2005 to 2010.
- The state's public schools consistently rank in the top ten for ACT, SAT, and Advanced Placement scores, making Wisconsin one of the "eight smartest states," based on the quality of primary and secondary schools.

But Wisconsin has also been an incubator for the national school choice movement, which seeks to send public dollars to private schools. Despite its high marks for public education, Wisconsin consistently ranks toward the bottom in one area: achievement by African American students. Currently, the gap between white and black students in Wisconsin is the second widest in the country, right after Nebraska's. This historic inequality has made the state—and particularly the racially divided city of Milwaukee—ground zero for a national battle about private school vouchers.

In the early 1990s, an African American state legislator from Milwaukee, Annette Polly Williams, a Democrat, became a conservative media star after she joined forces with then-governor Tommy Thompson, a Republican, to push a bill through the legislature that created the Milwaukee Parental Choice Program—the first large-scale voucher program in the nation to use tax money to educate students at secular, private schools. In 1995 Williams and Thompson worked together to expand the program to include religious schools.

Milwaukee's voucher program, which was specifically designed to serve low-income families, drove a wedge between civil libertarians, teachers' unions, and public-school advocates on one side and, on the other, low-income African American parents, their advocates, and conservative foundations led by the Lynde and Harry Bradley Foundation of Milwaukee. The conservative foundations made Williams a star. She was lionized by the *Wall Street Journal*, appeared frequently on national television, and went on the lecture circuit, collecting speaking fees from the Hoover Institute, National Conservative Summit, and other right-wing groups.

But Williams became disillusioned with the school choice movement when it began pushing to expand the program to all families—not just low-income, minority kids. "I knew from the beginning that white Republicans and rich, right-wing foundations that praised me and used me to validate their agenda would do it only as long as it suited their needs," Williams told the *Boston Globe* in 1998. "I knew that once they figured they didn't need me as a black cover, they would try to take control of vouchers and use them for their own selfish interests." She added: "Too many people in the voucher crowd exploit low-income black children."

As Williams's star sank with the school choice crowd, another African American leader, former Milwaukee Public Schools superintendent Howard Fuller, became the face of the school choice movement nationally. The Bradley Foundation endowed a special post for him—running the Institute for the Transformation of Learning at Marquette University—and he has taken up Williams's position as a media star and a staple of the right-wing foundation lecture circuit. But recently Fuller too has expressed angst at Republican plans to lift the income cap for school vouchers. "Please don't make it true that you were just using the poor to eventually make this available to the rich," he said at a budget hearing in Milwaukee.

School choice advocates also support charter schools. "We started by being the first state to have a voucher school, in Milwaukee," state representative Pope-Roberts said. "Now we will be the first state to … basically create charter school districts." While charter schools are public schools, and therefore fundamentally different from private schools in voucher programs, they can also be used as a tool to siphon off public school funding. When students opt out of neighborhood schools to attend publicly funded charter schools—to be immersed in a foreign language, a special arts or environmental studies program, or just to go to a higher-performing school—they take the per-pupil tax money with them.

Some school boards in Wisconsin and elsewhere have decided that the cost is worth it. Forty-one states have charter schools. In Wisconsin 206 charters were serving 37,000 students in mid-2011. By supporting innovative schools that must meet strict accountability standards in exchange for freedom from the regular rules and regulations, the school boards have created special programs within the public school system to meet students' needs and foster creative educational models.

The proposed legislation would also encourage the rapid expansion of virtual charter schools—online academies, which can receive the same per-pupil tax dollars as brick-and-mortar schools and could enroll students all over the state. Virtual charter schools started up in Wisconsin in 2002. As of mid-2011, Wisconsin had fifteen such schools, in which were enrolled nearly 4,000 students, most of whom have had most of their education elsewhere. Under the new law, and with many rural schools closing because of low enrollment, the virtual schools could become a much more significant part of the state's educational system. For a savvy business person, there is money to be made in a low-cost charter school venture.

K–12 education is the single largest budget item for each of the fifty states. So it stands to reason that privatizing education is the largest front in the conservative war on government. Liquidating public schools also fits into the conservative dream to "get government down to the size where you can drown it in the bathtub," as the conservative guru Grover Norquist so memorably put it. Hence the jarring attacks on teachers by Walker and his political allies in Ohio, Michigan, Indiana, and Pennsylvania.

But it turns out that drowning students and teachers in the bathtub isn't all that popular with the public. "I'm seeing this kernel of negativity and meanness in this bill," Milwaukee resident Lorraine Jacobs said in her testimony before the state senate education committee in Madison. As Lisa Scofield, a parent in Spring Green who teaches in the River Valley School District, put it, "This is not about education.

It's about money and control, and you are taking it away. How can you even pretend to strengthen education as you dismantle our state's largest democratic institution?" On the statewide expansion of charter schools, 120 people testified. Of these, only fifteen were in favor, and twelve of those had a direct interest in charter schools.

Republican state senator Alberta Darling, listed as author of the bill, was flanked by its real authors—representatives of state and national charter school organizations—when she introduced it. "These gentlemen represent a massive network," she declared. Todd Ziebarth of the National Alliance for Public Charter Schools testified that Wisconsin "fails to provide autonomy" to charters. David Hansen of the National Association of Charter School Authorizers said the charter school reform bill would make Wisconsin a better "policy environment," allowing more charters to open. If they failed, his organization could simply close them down.

The idea that closing a school is no big deal is perhaps the biggest difference between business-minded charter school advocates and the parents and teachers who came out to plead with their legislators not to destroy the public school system. "I don't want my children's school in someone's portfolio," said Scofield, objecting to the business lingo used by the bill's proponents. "I want it in my community, with local control." "I just wonder who is benefiting from this," she added. "Because it's not my kids."

"Charter schools are public schools," the charter advocates repeatedly intoned. John Gee, executive director of the Wisconsin Charter Schools Association, went even further, saying that children whose parents cannot afford private education need an alternative to failing schools: "Ultimately, this is a social justice issue," he said, to a chorus of groans from the other people gathered to give testimony in the hearing room. Gee was referring to historic racial divisions about school choice. After all, who wants to tell low-income minority parents that their kids should be trapped in lousy schools? The Madison Urban League's Kaleem Caire testified that the proposed legislation would make it easier for him to open a charter school for African American boys who are not well served by the Madison public schools. But, overall, Walker's education proposals faced opposition from both public school advocates and black leaders like state senator Lena Taylor of Milwaukee, who acknowledges that school choice is a tough issue.

"What we've done with this budget is to set up a secondary system of education with its own rules," explains Democratic state representative Fred Clark. If Wisconsin Republicans succeed in setting up their new statewide system of charter schools, Madison school board member Marjorie Passman testified, "those not chosen by lottery will return to the dying embers of our public school system."

"Add vouchers to the picture," Passman said, "and you'll actually have the poor paying for the rich to attend school."

That, in a nutshell, is the vision of Walker and the coalition of interest groups that helped draft his education policies. There is nothing remotely democratic about it. In fact, it is the brainchild of a network of national privatization think tanks and lobbying groups. Just listen to the buzzwords that pop up repeatedly as Republican governors and legislators across the country attack teachers' unions, cut education budgets, and privatize schools.

Governor Walker used the word *tools* with distracting frequency during a press conference about his education program. "We're giving our schools and local governments the tools they need" to make needed reforms, he said, which amounts to "a net benefit to school districts." If districts seize the tools and drive a hard bargain with teachers, they can save a lot of money, the governor asserted.

There is something funny about that word *tools*. It popped up again in Ohio, when Governor John Kasich announced a 16.4 percent cut to the state's education system. A press release from a think tank called Ohio Education Matters, which helped draft Kasich's plan, praised the governor's education effort, saying it "provides the right tools to help schools meet lower spending levels." Those tools include cutting teachers' benefits and "expanding opportunities for digital education." Digital education turns out to be the business of the group's parent organization, KnowledgeWorks, which markets a "portfolio of innovative approaches" to schools in seventeen states. On the cover of the January 2011 issue of the probusiness American Legislative Exchange Council's magazine, *Inside ALEC*, there is a large photo of a toolbox and the headline "State Budget Reform Toolkit." ALEC drafts boilerplate legislation and pushes a proprivatization agenda to state legislators around the country.

While there are good charter schools that work with local districts, independent charters that operate outside the control of local school boards are part of the toolkit of privatization and budget cutting around the nation. Robert Bobb, emergency manager of the Detroit Public Schools, has proposed a massive conversion of the city's schools to charters to deal with budget cuts. The rationale: Replacing all Detroit teachers with nonunion personnel would save the district money.

Nor are charters better. In Philadelphia a 2010 federal investigation turned up evidence of rampant fraud and mismanagement in the city's charters. The only comprehensive national study of charters, by Stanford University, found that only 17 percent outperformed public schools, 37 percent did significantly worse, and the remaining 46 percent were no better. Likewise, Milwaukee voucher students perform worse on state tests than their public school peers.

But cutting state education funds, especially if you don't have to pay union wages or benefits, especially if you don't even have to maintain a physical building, means big money. On education, Big Money has lined up against students, teachers, and local communities—from the inner city to little farm towns.

It is telling that in Wisconsin, just as the Republicans won both houses of the legislature and moved into leadership positions, top staffers left state government altogether to take new jobs—as school privatization lobbyists. "The voucher groups are the heavies now," said state representative Mark Pocan, a Democrat. "Bankers and Realtors have become the B team." James Bender, former chief of staff for Republican assembly leader Jeff Fitzgerald, is a lobbyist for School Choice Wisconsin. Brian Pleva, who ran the powerful Republican Assembly Campaign Committee, joined the indicted former assembly speaker Scott Jensen at the Washington, DC–based American Federation for Children, a spinoff of the Michigan-based group All Children Matter, which has poured millions into phony issue ads in state legislative races. All Children Matter was founded by Michigan billionaires Dick and Betsy DeVos. The American Federation for Children spent $820,000 in the last election cycle in Wisconsin—almost as much as the $1 million spent by the state's most powerful coalition of business groups, Wisconsin Manufacturers and Commerce. School choice groups form, dissolve, and then spring up again with new, patriotic-sounding names in each election cycle, according to Mike McCabe, executive director of the watchdog group Wisconsin Democracy Campaign. That way they can remain nonprofits, instead of 527s, and they don't have to disclose their donors.

So there you have it: money and political power bearing down on public school teachers and students with all the force of a mighty, well-financed, nationally organized lobby.

In May, Scott Walker delivered a remarkably inane speech to an audience of school choice advocates in Washington, DC. He began by reading from the Dr. Seuss book *Oh, The Places You'll Go.* (Anyone familiar with the politics of its author, Theodor Geisel, aka Dr. Seuss, could hear him groaning in his grave.) Walker went on to tell his audience at the American Federation for Children, including Betsy DeVos, that "every kid deserves to have a great education because they each have limitless potential." Never mind that he was in the process of pushing through the biggest school funding cut in state history. Walker also gave a shout-out to his disgraced former colleague in the state assembly, Scott Jensen, who was there in his capacity as adviser to the American Federation for Children. Since his indictment on charges of violating campaign laws in Wisconsin (to which he has since pleaded no contest in a plea deal), Jensen went on to play an instrumental role in connecting Wisconsin Republicans with national school choice groups' cash.

It comes as no surprise that Walker is a hero to groups that favor school vouchers or that his policies are not popular with teachers and public school advocates in his home state. But what did surprise people was Walker's announcement during his speech that he would expand Milwaukee's voucher program to other cities, including Racine, Beloit, and Green Bay, "because every one of those communities deserves a choice as well, and with this budget that's exactly what they're going to get."

"My only concern is that my governor went to Washington, D.C., to talk about this instead of coming to my district to announce it here," state senator Van Wanggaard of Racine told the *Milwaukee Journal Sentinel.* Republican senate president Mike Ellis went further, objecting to being blindsided by the governor's speech and adding that he did not necessarily support his governor on lifting the income caps for vouchers. Ellis added that he was shocked by the governor's voucher expansion proposal. "I'm amazed at this. I didn't see this coming," he said.

As the new executive director of the National Education Association, John Stocks, who is from Wisconsin, put it, "The taxpayers of the state of Wisconsin are being bilked." Stocks marveled at Walker's chutzpah: "For somebody who claims to be a staunch taxpayer advocate, he's a hypocrite."

Walker presented as a good thing his plans to create unlimited access to public school funds for parents who want their children to go to private schools. "Having no limits puts even more pressure" on the public schools "to do better," Walker said.

But Republican legislators are facing mounting pressure from constituents who don't like what they see. "It's pretty clear that voucher proponents are taking advantage of a new policy environment that resulted from the 2010 elections," said Stocks. "They are making substantial efforts to privatize education in Indiana, Ohio, Michigan, Pennsylvania, and Wisconsin." (That's why the governor of Pennsylvania joined Walker on the podium in Washington, DC, to accept the adulation of the American Federation for Children.)

The irony, Stocks pointed out, is that a recent evaluation by Wisconsin's Department of Public Instruction clearly shows that students in voucher schools don't perform as well as students in public schools. Worse, part of Walker's plan is to remove accountability for voucher schools by eliminating the requirement that students take statewide achievement tests. You wouldn't know about either the report or the testing exemption if you listened to Walker tout voucher students' graduation rates (but not test scores) in his speech in Washington or heard him extol the general concept of accountability: "Let's let every parent know who's succeeding and who's not." (How they will know, once Walker eliminates the requirement that voucher schools participate in statewide tests, is anyone's guess.)

What's the real goal of Walker's so-called education reforms?

"The real agenda is to dismantle public education through privatization schemes," said Stocks. That agenda is becoming increasingly clear to voters in Wisconsin—despite Walker's pieties about helping children and his claim that he reads Dr. Seuss to kids in classrooms three times a week.

Dr. Seuss, who once drew cartoons for the left-wing New York newspaper *PM*, would have known just what to make of Scott Walker. A lifelong champion of underdogs, "he had a keen eye for hypocrites, bullies and demagogues, and ridiculed them whenever he got the chance," as one of his biographers wrote. It would have been marvelous to see Geisel deal with Scott Walker's promise to improve education in Wisconsin through massive budget cuts and the transfer of funds to wealthy private school parents.

Patricia Schmidt, a white-haired elementary school music teacher from state senator Luther Olsen's district, told the committee, "Wautoma schools are bracing for the worst." Because of budget cuts, Schmidt said, she is driving to nearby Redgranite and teaching one hundred students over her regular load. "Our music program is very strong, and many of our students would drop out if they couldn't sing in the choir or play in the band, because they're not doing so well in their other classes," she said. Virtual schools would never fill the gap if her school closed, she added. She pleaded with the state senators on the committee to come see the students and teachers for themselves. Weirdly, bill sponsor Darling, who seemed distracted for much of the hearing, woke up from her reverie and thanked the music teacher for doing such a good job with her students.

Few politicians want to appear in public being mean to white-haired music teachers. But at the hearing, Republican state legislators had to sit and listen as their constituents predicted these politicians would go down in history as the people who killed their hometowns. Drowning government in the bathtub is all well and good until you're the one who has to do the wet work. So we got the bizarre scene in the hearing room: platitudes from politicians about "reforming education" in order to "help children," and citizens reacting with shock to the reality of brutal budget cuts and a vicious, predatory privatization scheme.

While Darling fiddled with her cell phone and whispered to her staff, Montello's Ligocki tried to describe what is important about local schools and their flesh-and-blood teachers. She talked about her relationship with her high school English teacher and mentor, Miss Maasz. When Maasz was about to lose her battle with cancer, Ligocki went to see her. "I asked her to tell me everything I needed to know about being a teacher in the few minutes we had to talk," Ligocki said. "She summarized decades of teaching experience with this sentence: 'When you walk into that classroom, your number one job is to love your students, and the ones who are the hardest to love are the ones who need it the most.' That sentence did more to prepare me for teaching than I could have imagined."

Ligocki went on to describe working in a school where half the students qualify for free or reduced lunch, in an area plagued by poverty and alcoholism. "Many of our students' parents can't or don't give them the care they need," Ligocki said. "I don't just teach my kids, I love them. I raise them." She talked about keeping extra food on hand for youngsters who are hungry. She told how she intervened when she saw that they were being abused. She explained how she earns their trust so they are willing to make themselves vulnerable and to try their hardest to learn.

Recently, during a training session on online teaching, Ligocki said she asked her instructor, a virtual school teacher, about his relationships with students. "He said it was mostly limited to emails and comments on discussion boards." The same day, she said, she went to a funeral for a beloved local math teacher, Andy Polk, a young husband and father who was killed in a tractor accident. Students and teachers stood in the rain for two hours, waiting to get inside the school for the visitation. "Students made huge displays with poems, pictures, and their favorite Mr. Polk sayings," she said. "The shortcomings of a virtual education could not have been more obvious that day."

And the value of a strong public school system could not be more obvious than it is now, as we face the prospect of losing it altogether.

FURTHER READING:

Apple, Michael W., "Grading Obama's Education Policy," *Progressive Magazine*, February 2011.

Barkan, Joanne, "Got Dough? How Billionaires Rule our Schools," *Dissent Magazine*, Winter 2011.

Ravitch, Diane, *The Death and Life of the Great American School System: How Testing and Choice Are Undermining Education*, New York: Basic Books, 2010.

Part 3 THE FIGHT BEGINS

WHAT'S SO FUNNY 'BOUT BEER BRATS AND CHEESE AND UNIONS?

*"WWFBD" = "WHAT WOULD FIGHTING BOB DO?" (SEE FOLLOWING PAGE)

THE DEMONSTRATORS REPRESENTED MANY DIFFERENT IDEAS & CONSTITUENCIES:

WISCONSINISM

INVOCATIONS OF "FIGHTING BOB" LAFOLLETTE, U.S. SENATOR 1906-25 & CHAMPION OF WOMAN SUFFRAGE, THE MINIMUM WAGE, CHILD LABOR LAWS, SOCIAL SECURITY, FREE SPEECH, ETC., ETC., CALLED TO MIND THE STATE'S GRAND TRADITION OF ANTI-CORPORATE PROGRESSIVISM.

WHO SHALL FILL THE PUBLIC STATIONS?

EDUCATED & PATRIOTIC FREE MEN? (SIC)

OR THE FEUDAL SERFS

of

CORPORATE WEALTH?

LIKEWISE, REFERENCES TO THE DISTINCTIVE FEATURES OF WISCONSIN POP CULTURE SITUATED THE RESISTANCE TO WALKER WITHIN THE VERNACULAR OF MIDWESTERN DEMOCRACY

CHEDDARHEAD

GREEN BAY   PACKERS

BRATS

FARMERS   WALKER'S ATTEMPTS TO CAST THE STRUGGLE AS URBAN ELITES VS. CONSERVATIVE COUNTRY FOLK FELL FLAT WHEN A "TRACTORCADE" JOINED THE DEMONSTRATORS ON MARCH 12.

WALKER WOKE A SLEEPING GIANT!

SOLIDARITY

COULD WE PEAS HAVE A VOICE?

CULTIVATE DEMOCRACY

WE SEE OURSELVES AS DEFENDERS OF THE CAPPER-VOLSTEAD ACT.*

JOEL GREENO

WHEN WE SEE WORKERS' COLLECTIVE BARGAINING RIGHTS ATTACKED; WE KNOW WE'RE NEXT!

PART OF THE GROWING OPPOSITION

*1922 LAW GAVE LEGAL STATUS TO FARM COOPS.

WORKERS OF WISCONSIN UNITE! YOU HAVE NOTHING TO LOSE BUT YOUR GOVERNOR!

Nicolas Lampert / Colin Matthes 2011 " justseeds.org " print based on 1969 / 1970 layout by Carla Critzy

AN INTERVIEW WITH BEN MANSKI OF WISCONSIN WAVE

By Patrick Barrett

Attempting to understand a phenomenon when it is still new, especially one that evolved as rapidly and unpredictably as the Wisconsin uprising, is always a risky proposition. Indeed, for those directly involved, the uprising presented an immense organizing challenge, if only because the ground shifted constantly, making it extremely difficult to plan even a day or two in advance. Nonetheless, reflecting on the characteristics of the uprising is worthwhile, even after so little time has passed since the massive capitol protests of February and March 2011.

The protests clearly reflected a mix of spontaneity and organizing, neither of which was sufficient on its own to explain their enormous and rapid growth but which together shaped the movement. One outstanding feature of the Wisconsin spring was its seemingly decentralized character. It was led not by a single organization or coalition but rather by a variety of different groups, organizations, and coalitions, not all of which were in contact with one another, let alone following a coordinated plan of action. Spontaneous mobilization, typically ephemeral, is difficult to sustain in the absence of organization and a strategic vision of an endgame. If organization was a necessary condition for the mass mobilization, do the people of Wisconsin have sufficient organizational capacity and strategic vision to sustain the kind of commitment, and fashion the sort of political orientation, needed to alter the balance of social power in the state? The Wisconsin uprising also turned the normal relationship between leaders and followers on its head. Rank-and-file union and Democratic Party members, as well as grassroots activists, were way ahead of their leadership in taking the initiative. Can this relationship be sustained? That is, will the grassroots continue to set the agenda or revert to the more normal pattern of taking cues from risk-averse union and political leaders inclined to dampen the energy unleashed by the protests and/or steer it in a less militant direction?

With these questions in mind, I sat down with Ben Manski in late April 2011 to get his perspective on the Wisconsin uprising. Manski is the coordinator of the Wisconsin Wave, one of several groups that played a significant role in the protests. Formed shortly after the election of Scott Walker, the Wave's central objective was to launch a campaign of sustained and broad-based resistance to the entirety of the Walker agenda, although the Wave did not anticipate the scale of the protests that exploded in February or the specific action by Walker, the attack on public employees' collective bargaining rights, that would trigger them. Manski, the executive director of Liberty Tree, a small nonprofit organization, had run as a Green Party candidate in fall 2010, vying for a state assembly seat representing Madison's progressive west side. His antiausterity campaign hit on many issues at the heart of the Walker agenda and was itself an impressive grassroots effort, enlisting the support of hundreds of volunteers from throughout Madison's progressive community. As Manski recounts, that legislative campaign served as a launching pad for the Wisconsin Wave, which also drew inspiration from the recent antiausterity movements in Europe.

In explaining the rapid and sustained growth of the capitol protests, Manski points first and foremost to the unusual strength of Wisconsin's progressive movement and traditions, which, he contends, are central to the state's identity. Manski asserts that the threat to that identity motivated tens of thousands of people to mobilize against Walker, even if they had no connection to unions. Manski also contends that conditions were ripe for some kind of major outburst, reflecting the reality that large parts of Wisconsin had been in crisis for some time. At the same time, he insists that the special character of Wisconsin unions was a factor; he argues that the state boasts more radical, or at least progressive, labor leaders whose social agenda is broader and whose experience in working within broad coalitions is more extensive than their counterparts' in most other states.

When I interviewed him, Manski was not concerned about the drop in intensity after the last major rally at the capitol in mid-March, viewing it instead as a welcome respite and pointing to a number of other actions that registered some degree of success, even if on a far smaller scale. Since then, however, the anti-Walker forces have suffered a series of defeats on a variety of fronts (most important, perhaps, over Walker's biennial budget). Indeed, in the short run, the effort to mobilize mass opposition at the capitol not only failed to prevent passage of the budget but ultimately fell far short of expectations, leaving many participants and observers deflated. Certainly, the spontaneous mass support and deployment of significant resources by state labor unions, which were crucial to the success of the protests in February and March, did not continue at the same level in the months that followed.

There has also not been much evidence of a clearly articulated strategic vision. Instead, the lion's share of energy was devoted to the short-term goal of recalling six Republican state senators, in the hope of denying Walker a majority in the state senate. But channeling energy into the electoral process carries the risk of further demobilizing the budding social movement. Moreover, in the absence of a well-organized mass movement, Democratic legislators as a group are unlikely to assume an aggressive stance vis-à-vis Walker, much less become part of a broader strategic effort to alter relations of social power in the state in a fundamental way. Finally, if the opposition to Walker continues to focus on elections to effect change, Democrats will not be in a position to reverse his agenda for at least two or three years, during which time a great deal of damage will have been inflicted on the state and its progressive social forces.

Still, despite these recent setbacks and missteps, at least some seeds for the emergence of a major progressive movement may have been sown. Those seeds may include an awakened political consciousness, drawing not only on the progressive traditions of Wisconsin that Manski stresses but also on a new generation of activists whose first foray into movement politics was the Wisconsin uprising. The seeds may also include a new surge of workplace organizing (ironically made necessary by the elimination of collective bargaining rights) that shifts power away from the top levels of the union bureaucracy to the rank-and-file and the labor movement's more progressive leaders.

Whatever the short term may hold, the task ahead is to nurture these developments with an eye toward building a social movement that breaks from business as usual by engaging in direct extraparliamentary action and placing far greater demands on the state's political (and union) leaders. Consistent with the view advanced by the Wisconsin Wave, building a social movement will also require the adoption of a long-term perspective on the process of social and political change, with an emphasis on forging a broad-based labor–community alliance with the capacity to engage in a sustained and targeted assault on the Right's social and institutional bases of power. Only then will the burgeoning social movement that emerged in February 2011 be likely to realize its full potential.

Patrick Barrett: Maybe the most remarkable thing about the Wisconsin protests against the Walker attack on public employee collective bargaining rights was not only their unprecedented size but also the fact that they grew steadily larger for over a month. What, in your opinion, were the key factors that triggered the protests and then fostered their enormous and sustained growth?

Ben Manski: I think it's important to recognize that, first of all, there was an awareness within not only the labor movement but within other movements that there were going to be significant attacks on working people in Wisconsin. There was not foreknowledge before February 11 that the attacks would come in the form of doing away with large sections of collective bargaining for public employees. But we knew it was coming. Conversations were happening. There was a lot of ground-work that had been laid, primarily for a struggle with the governor and with the corporate lobbyists in Wisconsin over the proposed biennial budget. I was personally at AFSCME's offices [that is, the offices of the American Federation of State, County and Municipal Employees] on February 11 at a meeting of a coalition that is now called Better Choices for Wisconsin, which is pretty much an alliance of advocates for seniors, for the disabled, for services for directly impacted communities. There was nobody from AFSCME at that meeting because the news had just come down that the budget repair bill would threaten the very existence of AFSCME as a union. But the fact is that we were having those meetings, and there were many other sets of meetings that were happening.

Personally, I had been involved in laying groundwork for Wisconsin Wave. I had run in a legislative campaign as a Green Party candidate in which my entire campaign was about mobilizing against austerity and corporatization in Wisconsin. And so we were ready for a struggle. The broader progressive movement in Wisconsin was ready for a struggle. I don't think we realized that it was going to take off that quickly. When I look back at some of the exchanges that I had with people, and some of our own materials that we had prepared for plans, we had thought that if we were successful, by May we might have 30,000 to 50,000 people at the state capitol. That would have been remarkable, but I believe that it was possible and also necessary, considering what I expected we would be up against. But of course we hit the 50,000 mark in a matter of weeks, not months.

I think that one major factor that contributed to the very quick growth of the movement and the protests in Wisconsin is that there is a much broader sense of the "we" for the progressive movement, for lack of a better phrase, than there is in many other parts of the country. Unions in this state have a broader social agenda that they have been promoting for some time. You have more progressive and radical labor leaders in Wisconsin than you do in many other states. You have many individuals who have done work in many different sectors of the movement. People who have history in the environmental movement will go and work on union organizing drives. I have many friends whom I met working in the environmental movement in the 1990s, I worked with them, and they are now in labor leadership around the state of Wisconsin: AFSCME, AFT [American Federation of Teachers], SEIU [the Service Employees International Union], in particular. And so you have this intersectionality, this crossover, that is common in Wisconsin. The family farm and the labor movements to some extent see themselves as two wings of the same movement. So it was not hard to motivate family farmers to come out in numbers to protest in Madison, and in fact some of the most significant protests early on happened in very rural counties. Not all of the alliances existed but many of them did. A third element is that this sense of a broader progressive movement in Wisconsin is very much wrapped up in the state's identity. We have the motto "Forward" on the state flag. There is a miner and a seaman on our state flag, and the state's identity, at least since the revolutionary era of 1848 [the year of the state's founding], had been bound up with progressive politics.

PB: At the same time, it's clear that Wisconsin has a dual personality, with both progressive and right-wing tendencies historically. The most recent [state] supreme court race [on April 5], with [JoAnne] Kloppenburg versus [David] Prosser, would seem to illustrate that once again. Even though Kloppenburg did infinitely better than was expected prior to the protests, and there was a huge progressive turnout, there was also a surge in turnout on the part of the right, turning the race into one of the closest in the history of the state. [*Editor's note*: Incumbent Prosser scored a narrow victory.] Explore that a little bit, as far as Wisconsin's character is concerned, because it sort of qualifies a bit what you're saying.

BM: The way to qualify what I'm saying is to say that the progressive movement in Wisconsin clearly not only has roots in our state's history but knows its roots, has a sense of legitimacy, and is very much bound up with the state's identity. So what that has done for the protests is that there were literally tens of thousands of people around Wisconsin who turned out immediately who did not belong to labor unions, did not have immediate members of their family who were members of unions but who came out because they felt personally threatened in terms of their identity and their sense of who they were as citizens of the state of Wisconsin.

And that is why I think you saw so much iconography that was sort of a spontaneous expression in the protests, and you continue to see it. You see the outlines of the state everywhere. You see people adding tattoos to their bodies with the state outline. You see the language of Wisconsin's progressive heritage very much as part of the protests. Clearly, Wisconsin has this dual personality, but I would argue that, over the long haul, looked at over years and generations, it's been a consistent fact that the progressive side of Wisconsin's personality has triumphed over the conservative side. And so we have had moments in which we've had a Scott Walker, or a Joseph McCarthy, or a Douglas MacArthur, but those moments don't actually last that long and they're not honored.

PB: Let's go back to the question of the labor leadership. Your characterization of it seems to be a little different than others'. It's typical to hear, in fact, complaints about the labor leadership (and this may be speaking in broad strokes), that it's typically conservative—both nationally as well as in Wisconsin—and that its inclination to move is actually fairly limited, and it needs to be pushed from below. Are you suggesting that that characterization is at least not altogether true—or maybe completely the opposite?

BM: That characterization is absolutely true. However, relative to other states, there are more people in leadership of both local and state unions who are not only open to direct action, and to strike action, but who actively support it and have supported it. I think it would be a mistake to offer ourselves the alternative of looking at the labor leadership in Wisconsin, saying either they are do-nothing sellouts in the pay of the CIA, as was the case for some of the labor leadership of past generations nationally, or they must be revolutionary unionists. Again, in perspective, I think that it was very significant that you had the president and leadership of AFT-Wisconsin pretty consistently strong in terms of mobilizing membership and in terms of advocating for more confrontational strategies. I think that certainly the leadership of independent teachers' unions in Madison and in other parts of the state has been incredibly important in moving the ball forward. The leadership of the firefighters' union, both here in Dane County but also now statewide—there's been a reform movement there and new leadership there—has been incredibly significant. So that's not something to be taken for granted.

I think that, to the extent that there have been significant problems with the role of organized labor in Wisconsin, many of those problems have to do with the relationship between unions in Wisconsin and the nationals and internationals. And that's not unusual. Frankly, from what I saw of the role of the national AFL-CIO and some of the international union representatives who were sent here, I think they could have been much more helpful than they were and in many cases were obstructive.

PB: What about the criticism that's often been leveled against at least certain unions and their leadership—that they very quickly and consistently, after the onset of this, were inclined to offer concessions?

BM: I think it was a huge mistake strategically for us to allow Scott Walker to point to the concessions that were agreed to and say, "Look, my strategy worked. I went after their power and they gave up on the dollars." But, more importantly, it was a big mistake, a failure on the part of some in labor leadership, to offer those concessions, because some of those concessions were not theirs to give. For them to concede on the budget repair bill, when elements of that bill had nothing to do with organized labor and impacted those who were dependent on Food Share and Badger Care—some of those people are union members to be clear, but mostly not—those concessions were an abandonment of key constituencies in the state of Wisconsin—poor people, predominantly people of color in many parts of the state, the very young, single-parent families—who needed organized labor to be there for them. I do want to be clear, and this is just my perception, that this has been a class war, and there's been a lot of fog in this war, so this may not be accurate, but my perception is that many people in the labor leadership never conceded on those questions initially. Those concessions were not made as a matter of consensus within the labor movement. In fact, those concessions were offered by a few—WEAC [the Wisconsin Education Association Council, the state affiliate of the National Education Association] in particular and AFSCME—and then the rest of the labor movement was brought along for the ride.

PB: Let me pull back a little bit and pick up on something you said, using the words *organizing* and *spontaneity*. A lot of people who have observed these protests in Wisconsin have interpreted them as being essentially spontaneous, at least suggesting that organizing played a relatively minor role in this phenomenon. And that seems consistent with how previous struggles in American history have typically been viewed by contemporary observers, an interpretation that historians have often shown later to be at least overblown, if not altogether mistaken. What is your sense of the mix of spontaneity and organizing behind the Wisconsin protests?

BM: In any situation like this, the primary role is always that of the individual deciding whether to rise to the occasion, so to the extent that hundreds of thousands of Wisconsinites chose to rise to the occasion, the protests were spontaneous. But looked at from the inside of this movement, it's very clear to me that these protests could have happened at any moment that sufficient resources were brought to bear to sound the alarm. Large parts of Wisconsin have been in crisis for a long time, and the crisis has been getting worse. From my perspective, I was confident ahead of February 11 that it would be possible to turn out these kinds of numbers and that it would be necessary to do so. I think that the reason why the protests grew so quickly is that the leadership of organized labor decided to get behind them very quickly. That's something that labor leadership has not done in this state, or in other states, to my knowledge, in recent years. When the protests started— and they were not started by state-level or international unions; the protests were started by students and by local union people—the leadership of the AFL-CIO in Wisconsin and various state-level unions got behind them immediately and put resources behind them. In doing that they were able to sufficiently mobilize an already existing base of people who were ready to make that decision to respond.

On the flip side, I think we should recognize why they made that decision in this case, as opposed to the last budget cycle and in previous cycles, in which clearly the interests of not only their members but also the broader public were at stake. And the reason why they made that call was because they sensed that the survival of their unions and their personal role in the labor movement was immediately on the line. It became that much more personal, I think, for many of them in that moment. So they figured that they had nothing to lose and they went for broke.

PB: So in the absence of the attack on collective bargaining, if I'm interpreting you right, they wouldn't have fought very hard and they would have continued to die a slow death, as has been happening, really, for decades?

BM: That's certainly possible. I think they would have fought hard, but I don't think they would have fought as hard, as quickly. I think it would have taken a raising of the stakes through a process of mobilization, and that's what I had in mind at that time. I had approached leadership of every state-level union, except for WEAC, prior to February 11, about the Wisconsin Wave to ask for support, and they were supportive. But when the attack on collective bargaining, and, more importantly, fair-share dues collection, came up, then it became pretty much impossible for me to have conversations with some of those people for a matter of weeks, and, as I found out later, it became impossible for many of them to have conversations with each other. They essentially dropped everything. I honestly think that there would have been a high level of commitment on the part of labor leadership to mobilizing around the attacks on the public sector, on benefits, on the UW System, on Badger Care, on Food Share, on farmers, on environmental protections. But their level of commitment wouldn't have been nearly as high so early in the process.

PB: You mentioned the Wisconsin Wave. How was the idea of the Wisconsin Wave developed? How was it created, and what role has it played in the ongoing struggle?

BM: The Wave takes its inspiration from the antiausterity protests of Europe in particular: Britain, Italy, France, Spain, Greece, Germany, Iceland. Many of those protests have been identified as waves of protests. In Italy the student-led protests against the corporatization of public higher education have gone under the name of the Anomalous Wave, and they took that name because a reporter referred to the protests as an anomalous wave of protests. Of course, the students knew that the protests were not anomalous, that they were a reaction to something very real, but they took that name on. In Germany they have the Global Wave of protests that has been inspired and led by graduate students across Germany. Through my work at Liberty Tree over the years, I've been in touch with students in particular in Europe and in other countries and have worked to connect them with people in the United States, with students and faculty and staff, as well as people working in communities, and to get more communication and inspiration. And, I'd say honestly, we've been very successful in doing that, in bringing the student movements in the United States into direct contact and solidarity with movements in other parts of the world.

The … Wisconsin Wave was developed as a plan of action [because] it was very clear before the election—before the election of Scott Walker—that that election would produce a legislature and a governor who would be very willing to dismantle everything that has made Wisconsin a model for the progressive movement, and that there would be a need for resistance, and that that resistance in Wisconsin would need to be understood in the context of the same kinds of policies being imposed elsewhere. So we took the name Wave, came up with a game plan, developed a statement, a call for the Wisconsin Wave of Resistance, which was initiated by over one hundred leaders—frankly, a pretty diverse group of people from around the state of Wisconsin— and came up with an organizing plan which recognized that the agenda that the governor has been pursuing is an agenda that was cooked up down the street at Wisconsin Manufacturers and Commerce, at the [Lynde and Harry] Bradley Foundation. Our belief then and our understanding now is that by making things uncomfortable for the people behind this agenda … we can actually cause them to back off. And I think that to some extent that's beginning to happen. That's where the Wave came from.

In terms of the role that we have played, there are many, many different formations that have come into being in the course of these past few months. I think it's fair to say that there are only two of them that were preexisting. Wisconsin Wave was one. The other one is the Better Choices for Wisconsin group, which used to be called the Revenue Coalition and included the Wisconsin Council for Children and Families, the Institute for Wisconsin's Future, the coalition for the aging, the disability rights action coalition, and others. But there have been many other efforts that have come together in the course of the protests as well. Many people didn't even realize that this process was already in motion. We decided to accept that and embrace it.

So what we've done is, first of all, [show] that we have staying power, whereas not every effort has. We have a long-term view. We have worked pretty hard, although not as successfully as I would have liked, to help to build the alliance that was missing on February 11, which is the alliance between activists of color, especially folks who are younger, people of my generation and younger, and leadership from organized labor. There is a point at which you can only do so much bridging. Both communities have their immediate struggles that they're in the midst of. But I think that we have at least gotten people together to the table repeatedly. We've helped to turn out different sets of constituencies for each other's protests. And we'll continue to do that.

And then the other element of the Wisconsin Wave that I think is significant is that we have really encouraged nonviolent direct action against corporate lobbyists and against those responsible for this agenda. Our first major action was a picket of Wisconsin Manufacturers and Commerce [WMC] at their state conference at the Monona Terrace on February 23. We also organized a march on WMC's headquarters earlier this month on April 9. Back to that question of building lasting alliances, the first mass rally that was a popular rally that was organized—not by unions but by a broader cross section of interests—was the March 5 rally at the state capitol that became known nationally as the Michael Moore rally but that in fact drew 40,000 to 50,000 people to the capitol who had no idea that Michael Moore was going to be showing up. And that rally, if you look at the footage, there were some amazing speeches from activists from Freedom Inc., from Color of Change, from UW–Madison students, Family Farm Defenders, union members, all kinds of people.

All the while there was another rally on the other side of the capitol, which was much smaller, and it was unfortunate. I think it was a sign of the way in which some people in the labor leadership nationally interfered with labor leadership in Wisconsin, because IBEW [the International Brotherhood of Electrical Workers] in Wisconsin was perfectly happy to join forces with the broader movement, and they were prevented from doing so. It was not their stage, and it [IBEW participation] was vetoed by somebody who's on staff with the AFL-CIO nationally. We had the go-ahead initially. We originally timed our rally to end when theirs was scheduled to start, and we were prepared to cut our March 5 rally shorter so that it could flow directly into the IBEW rally. We wanted to share stage and sound costs to defray costs. The main stumbling block, as I understood it from staff at the national AFL-CIO, was that they required that the speakers list for the Wave rally be vetted and that speakers guarantee that they would stick to AFL-CIO talking points. And that was pretty much a deal breaker because the main reason we organized that rally was to ensure that there were voices outside of those voices that had already been heard, that an understanding that the entire working class, not just those of us who were members of unions, was under attack. Their talking points were entirely focused on the collective bargaining fight, and they weren't interested in seeing anything that distracted from that issue.

PB: Whoever that person may have been, his or her perspective seems to be inconsistent with others within the state AFL-CIO. The We Are Wisconsin coalition seems to be embracing the notion that it's way beyond collective bargaining rights, and they're deliberately trying to create a coalition that includes a diverse set of constituencies. So it's not a monolithic state labor movement.

BM: This was not coming from anybody at the state level. These talking points were coming from the national AFL-CIO. That's exactly my point. If Wisconsin had been left to own devices, there would not have been any division that day.

PB: Has there been pushback as a result of that particular experience on the part of members of the state AFL-CIO who felt that that was inconsistent with their own vision?

BM: I was forwarded emails that showed that there were presidents of union locals in Wisconsin who were very upset, and I wouldn't say just emotionally upset but who were frankly coldly critical of that decision not to unite the broader movement. I think that in fact those criticisms to some extent were heard, or at least they took form in the way in which the movement has proceeded from that time. The reality is that there was a period in which the national labor movement was invested very heavily in what was happening here in a visible way, and they have since become less visible in Wisconsin, and there may be a great deal of funding still guaranteed for the labor movement here, and I certainly hope there is.

PB: Let me ask a question that sort of segues from that. What possibilities does this struggle offer for building a broad-based and enduring social movement—one that is inclusive of a wider array of oppressed communities in the state and that has the capacity to shift the social and political balance of power over the long term? And what are the challenges that such an effort is likely to confront?

BM: I'll start with the challenges to such an effort, because we have already experienced some of them. One of the challenges that we've confronted is that we are at a moment of emergency, of manufactured crisis, and in such a time there's not much time for deliberation. There's not much time for communication, and so people who had communicated actively with each other beforehand find that it's very difficult to have conversations now. And then you consider that, and you think … that in fact what we need is to have more conversations, more communication, new sets of relationships that are developing. You recognize that the nature of this situation as a crisis is in some ways making it difficult for lasting relationships to be built. On the other hand, the fact is that this is a crisis that confronts many, many different communities in many different ways, and many of those alliances are being built, but the trick is to make them something that is not so ephemeral but is actually lasting, and I'm not convinced that has happened yet.

For the Wisconsin Wave, we began a process of organizing people's assemblies across the state of Wisconsin. We had our first people's assembly at Madison Area Technical College [MATC] downtown on April 9 and 10, and we've reached out to some of these other constellations of organizing and asked for their involvement. Many of them had become involved already in that process. It was already broader than the Wave. But we've actively solicited involvement in organizing people's assemblies in other parts of the state as well for the coming months. The people's assembly here, and the future assemblies that will take place, are completely oriented toward building horizontal communication between people from different communities and different movements in Wisconsin, so that that communication no longer relies so much on those who are in the top levels of leadership [to channel] information down to their members. I'd say that the Wave has recognized that as a problem, and we've been working to rectify it. We've recognized that there's a need for more communication between different sectors.

PB: Is there dialogue or communication between the Wave and We Are Wisconsin, given the fact that We Are Wisconsin is explicitly trying to build a broad, diverse coalition, well beyond the labor movement? From the outside it would seem that there's commonality.

BM: I'm not entirely clear on the full agenda at We Are Wisconsin. My understanding is that We Are Wisconsin is a forum for a diverse cross section of organizations but not a formal coalition. That's what

I've been told by quite a few people who are active in that process. It's a place where different unions, different organizations, can come forward and bring to the table what they are working on and ask for support and cooperation, and Wisconsin Wave is now part of that communication process, too. But it is not a standing coalition, and it is not an ongoing campaign, so to speak. The Wave is very clearly organized as a campaign. We have unions, and we have organizations that have endorsed the Wave, but we don't promote that all that much.

So what, really, we've been focused on with the Wave is identifying needs and working to achieve the kind of lasting alliances that will be necessary not only for the coming weeks but for the coming years. And also to really go after power, to really centralize the question of power in this current moment, and centralizing the question of power means going after those who have power and also demanding democratic reforms in the process. If you look at the Wisconsin Wave's original six demands, three of them deal directly with democratization. There is the demand for a budget process that is participatory and inclusive and transparent, in other words, a process that is entirely unlike the process that happens every two years in Wisconsin, in which corporate lobbyists get together with the governor's staff and try to ram through a state budget. There's a demand for abolition of the doctrine that corporations are persons and money is speech.

And there's a demand for protecting the right to vote and expanding the right to vote in the state of Wisconsin. Those two areas or focuses—the focus on building a popular movement that is inclusive and has lasting power and the focus on winning greater democracy in Wisconsin—have been the Wisconsin Wave's hallmarks in the struggle.

PB: What do you see as the various possible scenarios in which this struggle might play out politically, if there are any endgames here? There's been some discussion about tactics, if not strategy. Fairly early on, during the protests at the capitol, there was talk of strikes, and even a general strike, as a necessary tactic needed to advance this struggle. And there's also been discussion, and people have actually pursued other kinds of actions or tactics, including recalls and boycotts. So give me a sense of what you think the pros and cons of these various tactics are and what negative consequences they may have, or how they might work in combination. It seems that not everybody is together—some are pursuing some, and some are pursuing others. What's your sense of that?

BM: Definitely, I think there's a sense that there's a division of labor in terms of the different roads that have to be walked at this time. My sense is that most individuals who have been involved in this broader movement respect the need for different tactics and are glad that there are others who are emphasizing a particular set of approaches so that they themselves can emphasize another set of approaches. There's this sense of interdependence that I think is very real. Not everyone shares that, but I do think that most people in Wisconsin do share that.

While I'm not working on the recalls personally, I'm glad that they are happening. And I have, to a certain extent, been counting on their success, and I believe that they will be successful and so far that's proving to have been a safe judgment—that there be energy and financing for the recall efforts and that some of the people who may take office as a result of these recall efforts will actually prove to be pretty decent progressive Democrats. The Green Party doesn't have capacity, doesn't have strength, in most of the districts. And so, as a result, it's pretty much a foregone conclusion that in these particular elections, we're talking about Democrats replacing Republicans. I know some of the people who are running, and, speaking personally, I think that they would be positive contributions to the legislature. So I've been counting on that happening. I know a number of people on the left who are supportive of the recalls but are not making that their main work. And my sense is that there are many people working on the recalls who are supportive of the street protests, the direct action, the economic boycott strategies, and so on.

In terms of the question of direct action, direct action comes in many forms, and I think the question of strike action is entirely separate from what's often called affinity group direct action, or confrontational direct action, nonviolent confrontational direct action. There has been some significant direct action in the form of sit-ins around the state. Some of that direct action has not been widely publicized. For example, there are high school students around the state who have held walkouts, not just in Madison and Milwaukee but in rural communities, and held sit-ins at their high schools. For example, Richland Center High School students basically completely captured the attention of people in southwest Wisconsin, and nobody in Madison ever heard about it. There is the fight against the foreclosure of a home in Madison that is led by members of Take Back the Land, and that is an ongoing struggle against this unjust foreclosure action by M&I Bank. You had the sit-in at Bascom Hall in which students sat in for much of the day and confronted the chancellor, in a way that she had not been before, with their opposition to her plans to establish a corporate authority to run UW–Madison, and they were joined by students at MATC and also by faculty and staff from both campuses, both institutions. You've seen repeated actions targeting M&I Bank, targeting Wisconsin Manufacturers and Commerce with pickets, and also zap actions involving people going into their offices and also picketing the homes of executives at WMC, for example. So that's been significant, and, of course, the most significant direct action was the occupation of the state capitol building itself.

That all said, I think there needs to be a lot more of it, and what has been very clear to me is that while there may be a willingness on the part of many people in Wisconsin to take on the risks and the sacrifice involved in taking direct action, generationally there is a gap in the know-how, so that people of my generation, who came of age in the 1990s and who formed and led the student antisweatshop movement and were, frankly, responsible for shutting down the WTO [World Trade Organization] meetings in Seattle, just in the sense that the direct actions that were organized were organized by people I knew and worked with, and I participated in that. Post-9/11, the practice of direct action in the movement nationally and also in Wisconsin dropped off quite a bit. So now you have people in their teens and early twenties who are having to learn these skills very quickly, and they're having to learn in a matter of weeks and months what we learned in years. And I think that there's a need for that learning process to step up. I honestly believe that if the level of independent direct action were to increase significantly in Wisconsin in the coming weeks, we would win. And there's no question in my mind about that. I think we may still win.

PB: Are you at all concerned that the moment has passed, that the energy and attention have dissipated, and that it might be hard to get it back or to refocus it in ways that will be effective?

BM: No, I'm not. I think it was necessary for there to be a period in which there was a chance for people to breathe. Because the level of activity for that first month in particular was so high that I think it was really inevitable that there was going to be a break. And I'm glad that it actually happened the way that it did, with a temporary win for our side, in that the attack on collective bargaining is on hold right now. And we have to recognize that, that as we're having this conversation right now, the main question that sparked this level of resistance is still a question. That's a pretty major victory, and regardless of whether people nationally or internationally recognize that, we won. That victory we have as of now.

I think there was a moment that was a very low point in terms of the energy We had 300 people come to a Wisconsin people's assembly and a 1,000 people march against the WMC, which in any other year would have been quite a success. But it was a moment in which there was a lull, and so we took a financial hit, a pretty significant one, in organizing these events. They were totally worthwhile, and I think the fact that we did them was very important to the broader movement, because people could see that there was this ongoing resistance. And since then, you've actually seen an increase in the level of activity in a lot of different areas around the state. You have the energy around the recalls. You have the energy around the recount [in the supreme court race], where essentially we stepped in last week for the Kloppenburg campaign filing for the recount. The Wave is a nonpartisan campaign, and Liberty Tree is a nonpartisan organization, and so we did not endorse anyone in that race, but Liberty Tree in particular has a history of working not only to protect the vote but also to safeguard elections after the fact. It became necessary last week to show that there was widespread public support for a recount in this exceptionally close and controversial election. And I think that the fact that we were able to do that on a day's notice, [when] it became evident that that need was there, and the fact that people responded and took it upon themselves to organize and to support shows that the energy level was building again.

Regarding the general strike vote, I got word that Monday night that the South Central Federation of Labor [SCFL] had voted to authorize preparations leading to a national general strike. I spoke to a number of people who are delegates to the labor council about it, and they were very clear about the meaning of that vote. The language of that resolution is exceptionally clear, and I myself have been a delegate to SCFL in the past, and I'm pretty familiar with who is there and how it operates. I got calls around 11:00 that night from journalists about it, and I explained to them, I think pretty accurately, what the vote meant, that this was explicitly a call for preparations leading to a general strike nationally, that the South Central Federation of Labor of course doesn't have the ability to carry off a general strike, but it certainly was a statement supportive of one. There were labor leaders in Madison, for example, Joe Conway of the firefighters, who made explicit their support for this concept, and my understanding is that the labor council in San Francisco followed with a resolution as well.

But within two days you saw a sort of dampening of the message about this resolution. There were labor leaders who were asked about it, and they were, to a last one, not individuals who were present at the labor council meeting. And I wouldn't say that there was a suppression of the resolution, but there was a lack of support for it on the part of higher-ups within organized labor. I've been asked by people in other parts of the country about what happened with that resolution. I've said to them frankly that it is true that the labor unions in south-central Wisconsin don't have the ability to call a general strike. And if there had been a wave of similar resolutions or calls in other parts of the country, not just San Francisco but also Boston, the Twin Cities, in Denver, in Pittsburgh, in New York City, and so on, that maybe that would have become a reality, as a real possibility. So, in some ways, I don't entirely blame labor leadership for their failure to get behind this call, because the lack of response from labor councils in other parts of the country showed that the rest of the country wasn't where Wisconsin was yet.

PB: How large are the stakes of this struggle? What impact might its success or its failure have nationally, or even globally? There are a lot of people who are paying attention to Wisconsin and even have said such things as "We're counting on you, how you go will have a major impact." What's your sense of that?

BM: How important this struggle is depends on who you are. If you are a Wisconsinite, then this is an all-or-nothing struggle. There's been a continuing tension here in Wisconsin between those of us who are from here and who have everything on the line, and those who have come to support what's happening here from outside. They have a clear stake and have been largely positive in their role, and they have a clear stake in seeing us succeed. If we fail, that will be a blow to the broader movement nationally, but it is not the end of the world for them. I think there are many, many, many people in Wisconsin for whom a failure on our part, for whom defeat would mean the end of the world financially, and therefore personally, for their families, for their future, and also for whom a defeat would mean an end of their world as they know it. Because, as I said earlier, progressive Wisconsinites do have a very strong sense of place and of tradition and history and have expectations about the future of this state, which have been put on the line.

Until a year ago, I think that most of us thought that Wisconsin would in the coming years become a world leader in green technology, that we would have increased investment in public infrastructure, that Wisconsin would not get caught up in corporatization and privatization schemes. So I think we had relatively high expectations, and that's especially true of working-class and middle-class white Wisconsinites, compared to expectations for other parts of the country. Now that we see that all that has stopped, and in fact that existing victories that we had won, or that prior generations had won, are at risk, it's a sense that the world can come to an end, and that's just a deeply emotional thing. So, for Wisconsinites, everything is on the line, I'd say.

For the broader movement, it's felt good for many Wisconsin progressives to see the rest of the country and many parts of the world recognize what we've known all along, which is that Wisconsin has been a heartland for the progressive movement for 170 years and that we have played a vital role in the labor movement, and the farm movement, and the women's movement, and the student movement in particular. Those are the ones that come to mind immediately. In terms of my own work, we have played a vital role in building a democracy movement in the United States. It's not a coincidence that at the same moment that these unprecedented protests were happening in Madison, citizens of Madison and of Dane County voted to abolish corporate personhood and the doctrine that money is speech, with over 80 percent of the vote. The same organizations, including my organization, were directly involved in starting the national movement to amend the Constitution. We continue to be involved in the leadership of that and also in helping to build the protests here.

So the long and the short of it is that I think that it would be a real blow to the broader progressive movement in the United States if we failed here, because the national movement will lose a lot of the institutions and traditions that have given them inspiration, ideas, and leadership for many generations. Organizations that I'm aware of whose founders were from Madison, or which were founded here, include AFSCME, NOW [the National Organization for Women], the Women's International League for Peace and Freedom, the Progressive Party, the Republican Party back when it was a radical party, the New Party, the Green Party. The Labor Party's largest chapter in the country was in Madison for a brief period of time. So, from the perspective of the broader movement, it would be a big blow.

PB: And, of course, Walker himself has the same sense from the opposite end of the political spectrum—what they can accomplish here will be a spearhead for a broader national right-wing agenda.

BM: It will be, and also that national right-wing agenda is an agenda to defeat the Left. And the problem that I keep on seeing rear its head is the reactionary corporate sector. Reactionary capital in Wisconsin and nationally understands the progressive movement better than the progressive movement understands itself in many cases, and [reactionary capital] is in many cases several steps ahead in terms of closing down our avenues for achieving change before we are even aware that they're there. And now, in the midst of this manufactured crisis, in Michigan they have brought it full bore to shut down local democracy. And they want to do the same thing here in Wisconsin. It's just one instance. In the case of the attack on unions in Wisconsin, it's very clear that that same set of interests has been aware of the role of Wisconsin unions, and also [of] Wisconsin organizations in providing leadership for the national progressive movement, and that's why they went after us.

8 EYEWITNESS: "THIS IS WHAT DEMOCRACY LOOKS LIKE"

By Dave Poklinkowski

The Wisconsin rebellion was in many ways a leaderless rebellion. The big unions tended to call the demonstrations (sometimes reluctantly, with a push from the smaller unions and their rank-and-file) and had the resources to set the stage. People turned out in numbers that exceeded several hundred thousand over two months. Indeed, two rallies were attended by 100,000 each. A mass movement was developing. The rally that packed the streets of the Capitol Square—shoulder to shoulder around the entire capitol—was amazing and unforgettable. I found myself marching for a while next to Ed Hill, president of the International Union of Electrical Workers (IBEW); I'm president and business manager of IBEW Local 2304. He had flown in because "this is the place to be, I wouldn't want to be anywhere else." The turnout was the kind that the forces of reaction and repression fear. But it was not my most memorable demonstration.

The power and the energy of the occupation of the capitol itself provided life-changing experiences for many; 5,000 to 10,000 citizens from nearly all walks of life were inside the capitol—warm and humid from all the humanity—chanting, "This is what democracy looks like." That was a moment that historians can only imagine, the sort of event from days long ago that they try to describe. The "people's house" provided warmth and immediate sanctuary from the outside cold; its architectural beauty and the spirit of the people inside pulled me and everyone else in. As a young cop imported for duty from Manitowoc said to me one evening as we were both taking it all in, "It's truly inspirational." And after a short, thoughtful hesitation he added, "And we know we are next." Solidarity, born through struggle, was tearing away the masks of the oppressors.

But if you want to know my very best day, it would have been one of the bitter cold ones, the kind you really had to bundle up for. I had learned from experience, so I had on thick wool socks inside my Sorel boots—for rallies on days like these, you had to dress like you were going to a Packer game in January. In these first few weeks of the struggle, it was the afternoon rally where the featured guest to be thanked was Tom Morello (aka The Nightwatchman from Rage Against the Machine).[1] My favorite band would have to be The Clash, so Tom's arrival was a very good thing for this struggle.

I've always thought that the national anthem should be Woody Guthrie's "This Land Is Your Land." We sang it in the public schools as kids in Manitowoc (another reason, obviously, for the corporate right-wing to cut public education). Can you imagine the people of America all singing this song at every sporting event instead of "The Star-Spangled Banner"? On this day the building trades were the featured organizers of the rally, as the unions tended to take turns providing organizational and financial leadership for the many rallies that were staged. The breadth and depth of the solidarity in the first two months of the struggle were truly amazing. There were no jurisdictional squabbles or chauvinisms; we were all brothers and sisters. We called each other "brother" or "sister," and we really meant it. Nearly 15,000 people attended this noon rally; a majority of the folks in the crowd were from the trades. Several musicians played two songs each and, fingers numb, retreated to make way for the next performer. Tom Morello cleaned up, playing five songs, and when he said his fingers were numb, no doubt they really were. With that, Tom played his last song and had us all sing, "This Land Is Your Land." Here we were, all kinds of folks, a huge contingent of traditionally conservative trades workers, singing as loudly as we could so they could hear us inside the capitol in Wisconsin and in the streets of Cairo. There were a lot of teary-eyed sisters and brothers. I was one of them, so much so that I had a hard time singing. Yes, this *is* what democracy looks like. It's what America is supposed to be.

In those early weeks of the struggle many folks in Wisconsin, individually and collectively, demonstrated that anything is possible. I saw people get up and speak from their heads and from their hearts, in

---

1   Protesters regularly chanted "thank you, thank you" to out-of-state participants, such as Reverend Jesse Jackson and trade unionists who came from Los Angeles [ed.].

public, as they have never done before and probably never expected to do. We exposed as myth the belief that the working class—indeed, the totality of labor—is incapable of recognizing its problems and doing something about them. The South Central Federation of Labor went on record as supporting a general strike, and its members immediately set out to research the issue. In all my years as a delegate, it was the first time I had seen the Fed firmly united and focused on a task without the usual jurisdictional tensions. The question of our collective future was before us, and we all knew it—and, most important, we acted like we knew it. In the first three weeks of the struggle, we were quite literally making decisions on an hourly basis. Like everyone else, I was exhausted but energized. (Wasn't it supposed to be *ten* days that shook the world?) In terms of possibilities, it was a time when truly everything was on the table, as local reporters quoted me as saying.

There were lessons to be learned, roads taken and not taken, and reasons for both. In the end, we were not talking about 1917; maybe it was more like 1905. We've got a lot of work to do—and we are busy working on it.

9

EYEWITNESS: "SPREAD THE LOVE, STOP THE HATE: DON'T LET WALKER LEGISLATE"

By Charity A. Schmidt

"Egypt's free!!!" my brother texts me that morning after he learns Hosni Mubarak has stepped down.

"Yes!!! Now it's Wisconsin's turn," I reply while sitting in the middle of a conversation that had heated to a temperature I would have never expected just twenty-four hours earlier.

It was Friday, February 11. More than fifty students, faculty, and labor and community activists were participating in a Labor and Working-Class Studies Project summit (what timing!). The previous night we had learned the bad news: Governor Scott Walker was announcing his budget repair bill, which included the now-infamous destruction of collective bargaining rights in Wisconsin. It was a comfort to be in the summit that morning, among folks who were similarly outraged at this unprecedented attack on working people. The summit turned into a discussion of what an affront this move was to labor tradition in Wisconsin and of possible tactics to stop it. The S-word (that is, *strike*) was flying everywhere that day.

By noon, when the meeting started, Walker had already made his declaration of war against public workers and the poor of this state, and he threatened to call in the National Guard if there were work stoppages, as well as fire any worker who chose to participate. We had known it was coming, that we would see massive cuts to union benefits and to higher education spending—but we didn't know the cuts would come so soon and with such arrogant force.

On February 1 a group from the University of Wisconsin–Madison Teaching Assistants' Association (TAA), including me, sat in the Memorial Union Rathskeller during a blizzard and watched Walker give the State of the State speech in which he declared that Wisconsin was now "open for business." That blizzard was perhaps an omen.

Our TAA chapter was already fighting changes proposed by university chancellor Biddy Martin. Her New Badger Partnership plan and proposed split of the UW System, which would have made all but the Madison campus second tier and accelerated privatization throughout, gave us all an early glimpse of the Walker agenda and its meaning. Graduate students, along with undergraduate groups like the Student Labor Action Coalition (SLAC), were already on the defense. For months we had planned to deliver a Valentine's Day message to the new governor. Again, the timing was perfect. I joined a thousand UW students and supporters as they delivered to the governor's office thousands of signed valentines reading, "I ♥ UW. Governor Walker, don't break my heart." This served as a kickoff event for establishing our presence at the capitol.

As we sat in that summit, it had occurred to us that we stood on the brink of something big. People were furious and ready to act. I texted my brother: "Might be a good time to visit me ... I have no idea what's going to happen. The word is spreading, the national guard called, could get crazy, or could get sorry. My bet is crazy."

By the end of that afternoon, emails were spreading about the Valentine's Day action, the rally days led by the AFL-CIO that were planned for Tuesday and Wednesday, and "call your legislator" information and talking points. Phone banks were being set up, and people were talking about tactics. The frigid temperatures eased somewhat that night and the rally-weather forecast for the coming week looked good—a sign that the universe was on our side. On Saturday I joined other students in hours of phone banking, and we packed the TAA office for a strategy meeting to prepare for the coming days. On Sunday several groups knocked on doors in districts outside Madison where Republican senators were thought to be susceptible to being convinced to vote against their party if enough of their constituency demanded it. A group of other sociology grads and I took a trip to the home district of Luther Olsen.

We knew the conversations would be tough; many of the people we were speaking to had voted for Walker. Our main message that day was that the bill was radically in opposition to Wisconsin's historic leadership on workers' rights, and that the bill's sudden introduction without a public hearing was nothing less than tyranny. Whatever might be said about the budget repair bill, in other words, it was the people's right to be heard.

That simple yet crucial idea—that the people have the right to tell their elected officials, face to face, what they think about various policies—resonated across the state. Senators' voice-mailboxes were full by Sunday night, and people flocked to the capitol Tuesday morning when the public hearing finally began. My brother also arrived that night, all the way from Bay City, Michigan. I ended a late night email to my favorite professor with, simply, "It's going down. See you soon."

On Monday we had swarmed the hall in front of Walker's office, dumping piles of valentines in front of his staff and yelling: "Spread the love, stop the hate, don't let Walker legislate!" (Of course, he was not available to accept the valentines in person: the young generation's greetings were rejected.) The scene was intense and provided some of the first photos that spread across the Internet and energized thousands, near and far.

The rest of that day was filled with meetings. We talked with university administrators about the repercussions TAs would face if they rescheduled classes and encouraged students to participate at the capitol (TAs wanted to move classes to the Valentine's Day action and were preparing for teach-outs later in the week. For one teach-out, students sent a Facebook invitation with the come-on "Sleep with Your TA"). We held an emergency general membership meeting, although none of us can remember exactly what transpired in that session—the recording secretary was out of town. But the night ended with a demand for Biddy Martin to make a public statement against Walker's attack, a demand she obviously ignored.

By Tuesday morning word had spread widely among graduate and undergraduate students: plan to bring pillows, sleeping bags, and toothbrushes to the capitol, and prepare for the night shift. The goal was to keep the hearings alive in order to prevent the bill from going to a vote. Thus we needed a continuous stream of testifiers. If students and the Madison community could keep it going all night, reinforcements (buses of union members) would arrive in the morning and keep it going all the next day. So we showed up—in droves.

Around 9 p.m., as the line to the hearing room grew to fill the fourth-floor hallway, the cochairs of the Joint Finance Committee announced that they would not accept any more speaker slips, and that Republicans would be leaving the capitol by 3 a.m. The hallway erupted as hundreds of people chanted: "Let us speak!" This was the first real show of determination by the protesters: we made it known that we were going nowhere. I looked around that hallway, filled with familiar faces, but the view suddenly looked very different. It was the collective face of a new movement. The spark had caught, and people were fired up.

Faced with a changed situation, Democrats agreed, perhaps reluctantly, that they would keep the hearing going as long as there was a line of speakers. We settled in for the night. People took shifts to nap, and others took shifts to alert nappers if their names were coming up. I lay on the first-floor rotunda, surrounded by my friends and colleagues (and even their children), many catching up on coursework or grading. I tried to prepare my next lesson plan. My students in a course called "Race and Ethnicity in the U.S." happened to be entering a new section: the civil rights movement. As they learned about the sit-ins and marches of the 1950s and 1960s, thousands would be practicing civil disobedience right across State Street in Madison. (I never had to teach that lesson plan, because their next class with me was during a teach-out, and I encouraged them to witness democracy in action at the capitol.)

My own slip to testify was somehow lost three times in the chaos of that night, but on Wednesday morning I woke up to the sunshine that was pouring into the capitol dome and filling the rotunda. The light had come to Wisconsin, the hearing was still on, the people were still speaking.

Part 4 LABOR

10 LABOR, SOCIAL SOLIDARITY, AND THE WISCONSIN WINTER

By Paul Buhle and Frank Emspak

The pervasive sense of solidarity expressed in high moments of mobilization during the recent Wisconsin protests fits poorly into most older categories of labor activity in the state, including strikes and boycotts, and hardly fits better with the history of left-leaning political mobilizations. Long-ago campaigns to elect the La Follettes (especially the original) or Milwaukee's success in electing four generations of urban reformers known popularly as "sewer socialists" to local office have some similarities and actual connections with the present, as do the Madison-centered antiwar mass movements of the 1960s and 1970s. In some respects even the Wisconsin Obama campaign of 2008 (especially the nomination process) bears some similarities. But not much more than that.

And yet, a curiously familiar laborist quality of the new movement, visible at all times, from iconography to chants and sing-alongs, has been unmistakable. Something important from the past, near and far, managed to survive and has now showed unanticipated vigor. The sharp decline of Wisconsin private-sector unionism, which accelerated from the 1970s onward, seemed to present the new governor and legislative majority with a moment they had long awaited: the prospect of eradicating their opponents' bases of support, both popular and financial. Whether conservatives overplayed their cards by rushing the case, or prompted a sleeping giant into wakened anger and determination, remains very much to be seen. For the moment solidarity has assumed a twenty-first-century character all its own, in many ways fresh, fascinating, and full of localist or regionalist features.

The expression of solidarity was both too pervasive and too elusive to be captured in any one set of graphics, even by the massive cultural production of YouTube videos, especially musical ones, attacking the Walker administration and buoying the struggle. The very diversity of the groups acting in concert was the single astonishing fact. By attacking the needs and interests of so many different constituencies simultaneously, the Republicans had managed to create bonds of unity where they had not been apparent only weeks earlier. Out of these fresh bonds came energy and creativity that might easily go down in the history of political iconography (including a wide-ranging behavior that might be described as performance art, like the repeated appearance of kilted firefighters with bagpipes, marching in and out of the capitol to wild applause). In what had to be a remarkable development, thousands, occasionally tens of thousands, of people of many descriptions roared, "What's disgusting? Union busting!" or responded to "I say union, you say power," with "Union!" "Power!" "Union!" "Power!" in a city with a modest labor history.

That the solidarity would be expressed most vividly of all, in sheer numbers of demonstrators, by educators of various kinds, along with public workers, was yet another remarkable feature. The professionals best known in other places and times for shunning formal association with horny-handed proletarians, choosing instead a guild status for their organizations, here merged into the crowd of electrical workers, snow removers, painters, and Teamsters with an unmatched enthusiasm. Many demonstrators held up signs handed out by members of the American Federation of Teachers that read, "An Injury to One Is an Injury to All." Quite, that is, as if they had been awaiting this moment for generations.

The events of the three decades or so leading up to 2011 would seem to pale against the longer history of unions and organizing campaigns, socialistic politics, strikes, and labor influences on mainstream Wisconsin at large. But such a view, encompassing the eclipse of the industrial base and, to a lesser extent, of the labor lobby in the statehouse, could easily disguise the subtleties of the changing picture. In this essay we seek to place a short history of public-sector unionism in Wisconsin in the broader context of the present movement's importance, highlighting specific struggles and their community support leading up to the days, weeks, and months of the 2011 struggle, and to present some highlights of seemingly unusual labor solidarity during the peak months of the protests.

The trend during the second half of the twentieth century, placing public-sector unions of many kinds—but especially educational, health, and correctional and/or emergency services—at the center of organized labor, has been inevitable, given the collapse of private-sector unionism. For many reasons, especially the dependence upon political lobbying to win and maintain union contracts, public-sector union success is also problematic. Most any state capital in the United States, outside deeply conservative zones, has been marked since the 1950s and 1960s by the spread of such unions. Their presence is linked decisively to social benefits and services badly needed among disadvantaged populations living under conditions of steadily growing poverty. These unions, long suspect within the mainstream labor movement, have been demonized with new vigor as enemies of the public good, and sometimes by Democrats hardly less than Republicans. But appearances can be deceiving, in many ways.

The story of the American Federation of State, County and Municipal Employees (AFSCME) offers a remarkably Wisconsin-centered case in point. During the first decades of the twentieth century, progressives had struggled hard to abolish the patronage spoils system (a system that Governor Scott Walker has sought to reintroduce through direct gubernatorial appointments, under an assortment of guises). Wisconsin public workers rightly feared, during the early years of the Depression, that the dreaded source of corruption was about to be reintroduced as a cost-saving device, hurling armies of employees out into the cold so that people with political connections could take their jobs. When the National Labor Relations Act of 1935 recognized union elections, the preservation of the civil service system opened the doors at least a crack to unionism in the public sector.

Efforts to organize employees had already begun in the state when meetings held in Madison during the early 1930s led to the creation of the Wisconsin State Employees Association (WSEA), the first such state employees' group in the nation. Prominent figures in the state's vocational education department stood out among its early leaders. WSEA made no direct claim to union status but promoted the advancement of its members and others working for the state, mainly through educational efforts and by lobbying legislators. The progressive Republican governor Phil La Follette, a practitioner of good government and concerned for public welfare during hard times, was naturally popular among state employees. As WSEA grew to about sixty chapters by the end of the decade, it was ambiguously chartered with the American Federation of Labor's "Federal Union" category, which required no contract with employers and little actual relation with the rest of a Depression-staggered (as well as largely conservative and faction-ridden) AFL.

The real success of WSEA in this period could rightly be called the first stage of defensive action, because the donnybrook about public employees' status, generation after generation, never quite disappeared from the legislature or public attention. Conservatives of both parties in the legislature, as well as businessmen and many farmers, refused during those days to accept the validity of unions for public employees at any level. The existing state labor movement itself, which had actually been launched by socialists in the later part of the nineteenth century, only gradually and grudgingly accepted public employees' unions as an important part of labor. Public support has seemed to surge and abate on the many related issues, always tied somehow to the budget and taxes. In Madison, where organized labor was weak but where most state workers inevitably congregated, a moderate public employees' lobbying group might be all that could be expected for the generation of founders.

But WSEA leaders aimed higher. Arnold Zander, a senior personnel examiner in the state Bureau of Personnel, acted as financial secretary, later executive secretary, and a one-man lobby in the legislature. Zander also spearheaded the project of a national union that he dubbed AFSCME; in 1936, the year of the sweeping reelection victory by Franklin Roosevelt that was also considered a great victory for unionization, WSEA became Local No. 1 of AFSCME, based in Madison.

For more than twenty years, victories remained local, that is, largely within the state of Wisconsin. They were fairly impressive, ranging from wages and hours to sick leave and overtime compensation. By 1940 steps toward the forty-hour week, paid vacations, sick leave, and such had been achieved. Throughout, an ethos of service to the state remained paramount; in the spirit of common cause the union welcomed management personnel as members. In turn, WSEA (and AFSCME) loyally supported civil service disciplinary proceedings against its own members when charges could be legitimated. On the other hand, until unionization became legal in 1966, actual membership among state employees remained limited and hardly existed at all among the best-paid white-collar sectors.

If the new AFL-CIO (the AFL merged with the Congress of Industrial Organizations in 1955–56) won anything important with its ardent support of John F. Kennedy for president in 1960, it was Executive Order 10988. Essentially validating federal employees' unionization, it prompted consolidation of trends already underway in a variety of federal sectors, themselves growing rapidly and in that way inviting all levels of public unionism. Wisconsin legislators, including a handful of old-time progressive Republicans, had famously jumped the gun a year earlier with the first laws favoring public employees' self-organization. Acting amid the grandest moment of national reform since the 1930s (and the grandest for at least two generations to follow), the Wisconsin legislature greatly improved on this in 1966, offering the most sweeping bill on unionization for state employees anywhere. Further improvements right up to 2009 established binding arbitration for many teachers and municipal and county workers.

Wisconsin Democrats took credit for these landmark measures, but their accomplishment should also be seen in the larger context of the progressive tradition: for the good of the state and its citizens, employees would be paid the salaries and granted the benefits likely to attract the most educated, enthusiastic, and talented potential public servants. It was an excellent deal for the future of the state, no matter how much Republicans and centrist Democrats complained increasingly about taxes and union-protected workers. How good a deal it was for employees themselves remained somewhat less certain. Salaries lagged compared with those in the private sector; the state always lost employees at various levels who could not live on what they earned; and, true to tradition, relative security (although Wisconsin was far down the list of states that guaranteed pensions) compensated for ungenerous pay. That is, until 2011.

Other contradictions were perhaps inherent in this kind of unionism, notwithstanding the bold stance that would come in early 2011. AFSCME founder Zander, who was cautious, conservative, and in tune with the AFL of the cold war era, proved unable to guide the union into the world of new opportunities and increasingly seemed to be a relic.

AFSCME meanwhile began to mirror the dramatic growth of new job categories that accompanied the rise of suburbs and their needs. The AFL merger with the CIO brought not only thousands more members into AFSCME by way of mergers of union locals but also a new sense that collective bargaining would win more than lobbying had.

Zander's leadership was near its end when Jerry Wurf, a young organizer of hotel workers, became president of AFSCME District Council 37 in New York City in 1957. The next year he successfully pressured New York mayor Robert Wagner into signing an executive order that gave city workers the right to organize at large, with elections establishing exclusive bargaining rights. Under Wurf, a civil rights devotee who helped launch the Congress of Racial Equality in New York State back in the 1940s, District Council 37 quickly became one of the biggest employee locals in the world. He led a team of reformers who wanted to push Zander out of office and won by a few votes (notably, Wurf's was the first successful challenge to a major union president since Walter Reuther won a bruising battle against the United Auto Workers' left wing in 1946). By 1981, when Wurf died in office and was formally succeeded by Gerald McEntee, the union had more than a million members. It had also put away a destructive tradition of red- and radical-baiting that went back to Zander's days and the ugliness of labor's own, often FBI-instigated, purges.

By the 1970s, as automation and the imports of some foreign goods, clothing in particular, sliced into manufacturing jobs, an era in organized labor seemed at an end. AFSCME became a key player not only within the AFL-CIO but also enrolled itself in some of the great civil rights struggles of the day. Indeed, Martin Luther King, Jr., had gone to Memphis, Tennessee, to support sanitation workers in their strike and paid for his heroism with his life. King's death set off union drives that brought higher wages and family insurance to a quarter-million new members, and, in return, those members had voting (and lobbying) power within a growing number of states. Unaffiliated state employee associations that joined AFSCME emphasized the role of African American public workers and the urgent need for pay equity clauses like those that had long been obvious in the paychecks of its women members. Victory in the first US strike for pay equity, in 1981, brought new members but also reemphasized the social leaning that made AFSCME unusual, if not unique, in the AFL-CIO. The parent organization was still run from the top down, and its top officials were still bitterly opposed to the social movements of the 1960s, especially feminism. They also remained rabidly in favor of the Vietnam War and allergic to affirmative action of all kinds.

Indeed, McEntee led the struggle in 1995 to oust the AFL-CIO leadership team of George Meany's incompetent and fiercely hawkish successor, Lane Kirkland. Kirkland had surrounded himself with union presidents who were making CEO-level salaries and were out of touch with their members. He had been long rumored to have gained his status as leader-in-waiting way back in the 1950s through intelligence agency influence. Out went Kirkland and his own intended successor, out went the anti-immigrant bylaws in place since the founding of the AFL in the nineteenth century, and in came a breath of fresh air. But unionism had slipped too far down to recover in the short run and fell further still in the decades that followed. However, the few major gains were made most often by public employee unions, along with labor organizations serving health workers (and travel-related employees, including hotel and casino workers). Within the AFL, staggered by defections of major unions at the end of the twentieth century, McEntee and AFSCME looked larger than ever, and this provided a bigger target for Republicans aiming at state budgets and catering to rightward-leaning, hitherto traditionally Democratic, voters. If this history seemed distant from Wisconsin in 2011, McEntee's appearance in the rotunda on February 15, the very first national labor leader to physically appear on the scene, confirmed its relevance.

A few days earlier Randi Weingarten of the American Federation of Teachers (AFT) had appeared in Madison, but only to visit the University of Wisconsin campus and the Teaching Assistants' Association there (and purportedly to urge TAA members to accept concessions necessary to preserve their contract). Perhaps more accurately known in the twenty-first century by its slogan, "a union of professionals," the AFT soon proved to be second- or third-most important, after AFSCME, in the number and variety of signs distributed during the mobilizations and in the number of self-representing members. To the degree that the TAA proved tactically central to the struggle, so did the AFT.

The first Wisconsin AFT local went back all the way to 1933, but the union experienced poor luck in recruiting local primary and secondary school teachers, who stayed out of labor unions for generations and finally shunned the AFT for its competition, Wisconsin entities affiliated with the National Education Association. More precisely, the NEA was a guild that was becoming a union during the 1970s and 1980s, and was better suited for the complications of laws and customs without ceasing to be militant in its own, often peculiar, ways.

Teacher unionism at large offers a twisted history with interesting consequences for Wisconsin. Schoolteachers in New York State, especially those in the Greater New York of the 1930s and 1940s, had affiliated in considerable numbers with the Teachers Union, which pioneered Negro History Week and otherwise stood at the forefront of socially concerned unionism. Destroyed by cold war attacks, the TU yielded at last to the AFT, a more conservative body that was dominated by its New York affiliate, the United Federation of Teachers. The AFT, like AFSCME, grew rapidly during the 1960s and 1970s, in part by using militant tactics, including strikes, and in part by wheeling and dealing with local and state politicians. The AFT failed to spread much into Wisconsin for several reasons, among them, the union's hawkish support for the Vietnam War and the racially divisive rhetoric of Albert Shanker, the AFT's dominating (and domineering) president until his death in 1997.

The TAA, which never boasted more than three to four thousand members but had great enthusiasm for politics and reform, made the difficult choice of affiliating with the AFT in 1974. Wisconsin progressives were constituting a growing presence in the AFT, much to the dismay of Shanker's team—by that time a central locus of neoconservatives within labor—and the progressives actually were successful in spreading the solidarity gospel (Wisconsin's distance from New York was often cited as a key factor in gaining them the autonomy they needed). The TAA's dramatic success, beginning with an initial contract won in the spring 1970 strike with the help of Teamster Local 695's refusal to cross a picket line, was for a long time an anomaly. Eventually it inspired unionism on other Wisconsin campuses, mainly among college teachers and academic staff within the state system. After being lobbied for decades, the state legislature finally granted the TAA bargaining rights in 2009, a move that was followed by strong votes for unionism on six campuses.

Otherwise, the AFT spread in Wisconsin mainly among professionals with advanced degrees, including the last large group of unorganized state employees, the Fiscal and Staff Services bargaining unit, along with public defenders. As a half-dozen unions raced to service the one rapidly growing field evidently ripe for unionization, the state AFT could claim about 17,000 members when the 2011 crisis began, not a huge number but a powerhouse of potential energy in a critical location.

In Wisconsin the AFT has been overshadowed in numbers, if not always in influence, by the NEA, which by 2011 represented nearly 100,000 Wisconsin teachers and support professionals, from librarians to bus drivers and cooks and including some employees of prisons and assorted other state institutions, as well as faculty and staff of the state technical college system. The organizations that eventually would affiliate with the NEA had represented teachers and school administrators even longer than AFSCME had. These state organizations had been started in the mid-nineteenth century and drifted toward unionism. After passage of a collective bargaining law for public employees, the association evolved into a proactive teachers union and in 1972 changed its name from the Wisconsin Education Association to the Wisconsin Education Association Council. Later, WEAC expanded its membership to include educational support staff, as well as education and information professionals in the Wisconsin Technical College System and elsewhere. In other words, WEAC and the AFT competed for members in several sectors for decades, and not always in an amiable fashion.

By the early 1970s teachers were heavily impacted by the social movements of the day—civil rights, antiwar, and feminism, to mention only a few. Historically reluctant to take direct action but not without a cadre of activists (especially, but not only, in Dane County), teachers showed a new militancy with dozens of strikes and sick-outs. Two were especially important, in different ways. A 1974 strike in little Hortonville galvanized the ranks and brought a legal defeat that led to a sort of political victory for teacher unionism. A teachers' strike in Madison just two years later prepared the way for a major expression of solidarity around the newspaper strike of 1977–80 and, even more, around the strikers' own daily newspaper, which took a run at displacing the *Capital Times* as the progressive voice of a city deeply influenced by contemporary social movements.

In a broader sense the two strikes were predictive of events in 2011.

Teachers had historically been taken for granted, even perhaps by liberals (and certainly by Democrats), as their low salaries demonstrated. Support of teachers by a wider public, during conflicts with cities and school boards, marked a kind of preliminary defense of the social state; what was happening then became clear decades later as the attack upon state social services accelerated. The existence of state and local safety nets owed something to the social movements for change of the 1960s and 1970s, and the assistance had survived despite all the backward steps of the Reagan years and the Clinton cut in welfare services. In the twenty-first century, holding on to the safety net would constitute a modern version of La Follette's vision.

We need to mention another chapter in the history of Wisconsin teachers unions. In 1959 the legislature passed the Municipal Employee Relations Bill, which set the stage for the Milwaukee Teachers' Education Association to become the state's first certified bargaining agent for teachers. Although strikes, as such, remained illegal, teachers in various localities increasingly pressed their luck as time went on, in part because the law against public employees' striking contained no specific penalties. The formation of the Wisconsin Education Association Council was, then, both an effect of teachers' determination and cause for further militancy. WEAC also collected dues that went toward paying lobbyists to represent teachers before the legislature, and the council claimed major political victories by the mid-1970s.

No one would have expected teachers in little Hortonville, in conservative Outagamie County, west of Green Bay, to take the next step. But they had little choice. After months of discussion the school board made a paltry take-it-or-leave-it offer, and when teachers chose to leave it, the board immediately announced, on April 2, 1974, that it had fired the teachers.

Family members and other teachers from the area, including Green Bay, as well as from Madison (including many from the TAA), Milwaukee, and elsewhere, showed up on picket lines and were met by deputy sheriffs in helmets and carloads of strikebreakers—not to mention the thugs of the Hortonville Vigilante Association—who harassed the picketers. The boldest of the teachers staged a sit-in and were hauled off to jail in Appleton, Joe McCarthy's hometown. By April 1974 the strike was national news and managed to embarrass the state superintendent of schools, who was forced to admit that uncertified, unqualified teachers were now in classrooms. The Hortonville Education Association had already moved into legal action as soon as a judge limited picketing, prompting the first call for something like a general (teachers) strike in the state within modern times. When WEAC asked its members to ratify a general strike of all state teachers on April 26, the motion actually failed, 4–1.

The decisive defeat of Hortonville teachers came two years later, when the Supreme Court ruled that teachers could, indeed, be fired for rejecting a school board offer. But the thirty-odd local strikes during 1972–74, most lasting no more than two weeks, did win "just cause" requirements for firing and real upgrades in both salary and insurance. Typically, in the bargaining dance, teachers threatened to strike, school boards threatened to seek injunctions with penalties, and they resumed bargaining until they reached agreement. Binding arbitration, which the state legislature made a requirement in 1977, came with a common recognition of the unnecessary complications and limitations of this process.

The final reminder of a need for the new law came, perhaps, in the early months of 1976, within a few miles of the Wisconsin Capitol. During the bitterly cold first days of January, Madison teachers canceled classes after months of fruitless negotiations with the school board. Persistently low salaries (base pay: $8,800), teacher evaluations, health insurance, and class size all were on the table. Informational picketing had commenced in early December 1975, and a sick-out of more than half the roughly 2,000 teachers followed, spearheaded by Madison Teachers Incorporated (MTI), a local forerunner of WEAC. This was the first time schools in Madison had been closed by a labor action. To their own surprise, perhaps, almost 90 percent of the teachers did strike when the new term began on January 5. They stayed out for ten days, winning improvements almost across the board and, by most estimates, pushing the state toward binding arbitration. It was said, in later years, that the MTI strike, along with a public employees' action of the next year—a fifteen-day state strike beginning July 3, 1977, and ending with arbitration—were the last to break much new ground for decades to come in most parts of Wisconsin.

No doubt the famously divisive Madison newspaper strike of the same year began as a defense. Papers across the United States, flush in advertising money, moved to computerize typesetting, which promised higher profits. The typesetters of the International Typographical Union (ITU), the oldest continuous union in the nation, seemed doomed one way or the other. Madison Newspapers, Inc., was set up in the 1940s to join two dailies, one a Republican or conservative morning paper, the other a liberal and sometimes progressive evening paper, so that they shared costs and split profits on some operations. By the 1970s the two papers were jointly owned by Lee Enterprises, a small national chain, although a foundation attached to the *Capital Times* operated somewhat independently. Management bought the new cold type equipment secretly and meanwhile moved the newspaper plant from downtown to a railroad spit on the margins, thus making it impossible to shut the papers down with a picket line in the event of a strike. The firings of typesetters began in March 1977 in violation of seniority rights, and events moved along toward a bitter strike. In October the five unions at the two papers struck simultaneously and coordinated with each other in impressive fashion, with enthusiastic support of a significant portion of the public. Publication of the dailies, with replacement staffs, nevertheless continued.

Having effectively lost the strike, after a few months the strikers shifted from producing a weekly strike paper to putting out a full-blown daily, physically small compared with its two competitors but full of life. Scooping the big papers, developing editorial and artistic talent (the nationally known labor cartoonist Mike Konopacki began there), the *Madison Press Connection* evolved into one of the very few cooperatively owned and operated papers in the nation. Few in Madison were unaware of the irony that the *Capital Times* had itself originated in 1917 as a left-leaning, antiwar daily.

The *Press Connection* constituted a unique experiment, even in a state with a strong tradition of working-class socialists, third-party progressives, and assorted small-scale cooperative enterprises. Workers in each of the new daily's departments undertook their own supervision, made their own decisions, and sent representatives to the production council that ran the paper; workers in all departments (except classified advertising clerks, a sort of piecework job with growth potential) earned exactly the same wage. Most of all, however, the paper would be remembered as the very soul of solidarity. It ardently supported nurses, cab drivers, and others facing probable strikes, exposing the tricks of management. The paper presented itself as the spiritual center of the administration of Madison mayor Paul Soglin, and it ardently supported Soglin's probable successor, James Rowen (not so incidentally, he was the son-in-law of Senator George McGovern, and later a luminary at the *Milwaukee Journal-Sentinel*, which by spring 2011 offered more dirt on Scott Walker than any other Wisconsin daily).

The *Press Connection* could not survive the defeat of Rowen by a bland University of Wisconsin professor whose campaign coffers had been filled by both political parties, the banks, and real estate interests in town. A new era had thus opened in Madison, not an especially good one for labor solidarity or social solidarity of any kind, despite the active sympathies of members of the Communications Workers of America, AFSCME, and teachers unions for the *Press Connection* and other labor causes. In Milwaukee and Madison the civil rights movement had peaked some years earlier, the power of the state's Republicans grew during the 1980s and 1990s, and the Democrats' base narrowed with the downward slide of private-sector unionism—all factors that threatened to bring what finally arrived in the governor's office, with heavy out-of-state corporate backing, in early 2011.

Meanwhile, the era of defensive strikes was now well underway in Wisconsin, even if some existing unions, and especially the building trades, showed precious little solidarity toward other unionists. The precipitous decline of production left existing factory workforces and their unions eager to make concessions in order to discourage corporations from moving elsewhere. Too often these workers and their unions realized afterward that plans had already been made and concessions had only lowered the cost of labor until the company closed the plant.

But a wider story of these years is less frequently told and still less understood. As the traditional unions weakened, progressives who had experience in the civil rights, antiwar, and environmentalist movements of the 1960s and 1970s arrived at new positions of influence, not only in their own unions but more prominently in local or regional labor federations. The poisonous conservatism of the leaders of the South Central Federation of Labor toward the newspaper strike prompted a kind of spiritual revolt, led by the former newspapers' pressmen and the TAA, that catapaulted TAA leader David Newby into the presidency of the SCFL in 1982.

Newby brought in his own team and set about establishing a new sense of solidarity—long a favorite word of unionists, it had been given new emphasis by Polish Solidarity. He established teams of volunteers who would drive to, say, Minnesota (for the Hormel [P-9] strike of the mid-1980s) or Illinois (for the Staley strike of the mid-1990s), among other actions. Opposition to the repugnant hawkishness of AFL leaders also prompted a fresh and authentic globalism, brought home by the new community alliances with Dane County minorities, including undocumented immigrants, through the work of the Interfaith Coalition for Worker Justice of South Central Wisconsin. The Labor Temple Hall, in the hands of progressive leadership, increasingly opened its doors to community groups but also to labor militants of national stature. The SCFL's own paper was revived as the labor press nationally swooned, while SCFL leaders reached out to local and regional unions that had long been known for their conservatism but were now faced with their own generational shift, which sometimes made them open to new directions. Madison labor activists, likewise, partnered with students at the UW, Madison Area Technical College, and local high schools, and were at the forefront of the nationwide antisweatshop movement. As the organization known locally as the Fed (the SCFL) became the South Central Wisconsin Labor Federation in a consolidation move, and as Newby himself moved on to become president of the state Federation of Labor in 1993, a new day dawned. Certainly it was late, but optimists and idealists hoped that perhaps it was not too late for revival.

Something similar happened in Milwaukee. Bruce Colburn and John Goldstein, former bus drivers known for their long-standing ties to the civil rights movement and Jobs with Justice, a workers' rights coalition, worked with increasing success to revive and transform the Milwaukee County Labor Council. They and their supporters determinedly built alliances with community groups but also among union locals that had often been out of touch with each other in recent decades (charity golfing events held for union officials typified the state of relations in many places, along with election-season rallies and fund-raisers). Labor Day social events became both popular and inclusive, an apt symbol of intent.

Meanwhile the new reform leadership of the national AFL-CIO of the mid-1990s had begun pushing for innovation, with central labor councils taking the lead. Milwaukee's central labor council, the Milwaukee County Labor Council (MCLC) won guarantees that employers at hotels built with public subsidies would remain neutral when workers tried to organize; in the new century, the MCLC mobilized thousands, in alliance with civil rights and other groups, to march around the site of a new convention center and baseball stadium. Demanding and winning agreement on construction there, as well as promises to hire more minorities, they gained or regained something of the labor foothold that was being lost with the plant closings. A few years later Colburn became a leading figure in the AFL-CIO, implementing the "New Alliance" plan that coordinated national unions, local federations, and state federations into a coherent strategy for the new economy and shifting political tides. The avid participation of the MCLC in the local immigrant rights demonstrations that began in 2006 offered a vindication of sorts but also a promise.

As the events of spring 2011 showed so clearly, many obsevers have too easily and precipitously closed the book on Wisconsin's organized labor, even within the private sector. A workforce with increasing numbers of women and nonwhite workers, the strong national trend since the 1960s, impacted the remains of industrial production, especially "little steel" (once centered in a north-south line from Kenosha to Waukegan, Illinois), which encompassed everything from automobiles to motorcycles (the famed Harley Davidson facility in Milwaukee). The demography was changing in another way too, but it affected neighboring Minnesota and Iowa-Nebraska much more heavily than Wisconsin: immigrant workers were arriving in large numbers and accounting for percentages of the workforce not seen in almost a century, largely a result of the expansion of meatpacking facilities.

In larger Wisconsin cities, where large numbers of Mexican immigrants worked in nonunion sectors, especially retail and services of all kinds, a new kind of solidarity nevertheless emerged with the new century. May Day, a hallowed holiday in the old German American cities and towns where socialists once held office, became (as it did in Madison) Immigrant Rights Day, and not only in Milwaukee. Turnouts were larger than those for any May Day since the 1940s, and sometimes included at least a smattering of union members and officials. The estimated 100,000 participants in the Milwaukee May Day/Immigrant Rights Day of 2011 had to be the largest labor turnout in the state in recent memory, just after the 125,000 in Madison in mid-March.

Doubtless, defensive strikes sometimes had a way of bringing out the oldtimers for one last courageous stand—as well as sending union leaders scurrying for any settlement that might keep the jobs from moving away. The May 14 event in Madison had perhaps 8,000 participants, at least half of them bused in by AFL-CIO affiliates from the four corners of the state and especially from distant northwest Douglas County, where militancy had remained an undying tradition. Who were the labor loyalists from out of town? Largely middle-aged men and women, holding up union signs or marching with contingents, veterans, often survivors, of union locals on the verge of vanishing.

This demographic fact or coincidence did not necessarily militate against a larger sense of solidarity. People in their early sixties were, after all, part of the largest US generation in history, and participants, or at least contemporaries of those who participated, in the social struggles of the 1960s and 1970s, from civil rights to women's rights, that had pushed the nation leftward the last time around. Baby boomers could easily be around for several more decades, many of them fighting the good fight. They are matched, in age and to some degree in experience, with Madison radicalism's home guard, the survivors of a vanished (or at least badly aged) New Left that has suffered defeats on dozens of fronts, from war protests to school funding, but are more resilient than anyone might have expected.

In one key way, the Capitol Square demonstration of June 14 can be seen as an ending, or preparation for an ending, of sorts. Before the last speaker took the mic, the Wisconsin Supreme Court had ruled (hastily, according to the chief justice), with evident bias, that the collective bargaining provisions of January had been legal; early on the morning of June 16, the state assembly passed the hated budget itself, and soon the state senate followed suit. By the end of the month all measures had become law, barring any future legal effort in the federal courts to overturn one or another part.

A crowd of perhaps 10,000 had gathered for the rally on June 14, but the state president of the AFL-CIO, Phil Neuenfeld, and the president of WEAC, Mary Bell, had seemingly placed all labor's eggs in a single basket: the recall effort. Any notion of job action or a sustained, public protest movement or demonstrations and occupations appeared to have evaporated, for now at least.

The history of public unionism in Wisconsin might thus be said to have come full circle. Public-sector unions, AFSCME and teachers unions in particular, had begun essentially as lobbying agencies, seeking to enforce or improve somewhat the existing laws and practices while advancing toward something like real unionism only after decades of political effort. Along with later public service arrivals like the Service Employees International Union and the Laborers Union, these organizations usually hoped the Joint Finance Committee of the Wisconsin Senate and Assembly would reach an agreement on contracts that the governor would sign. Although they had sometimes used more militant lobbying efforts, occasional sick-outs, and even strikes over the years, in 2011 public employee unions had not contemplated serious preparation for a different scale of events and mobilization. Faced with opposition driven by ideology, the unions concluded that lobbying had lost its relevance.

The months of efforts devoted to getting union members and supporters to events at the capitol and around the state were, then, no small matter. Buses were chartered and paid for; meanwhile labor activists went around the country to carry the message and garner more support (Firefighters' leader Mitchell Mahon was a crowd-pleasing favorite across the country). Union activists, including those reactivated after years or decades of detachment, proved themselves in it for the long haul, badgering the governor with signs and shouts wherever he spoke in public. The recall effort set another phase in motion, with some help from across state lines but mainly relying upon unionists and friends to knock on doors, make phone calls, and otherwise seek to get out the vote against the huge surge of outside money and Republican propaganda.

Labor had long supported Democrats but rarely with this degree of urgency. Arguably not since the 1940s had labor pushed so hard against Democrats' timidity and their get-along-go-along collegiality toward their Republican counterparts. Militant industrial unionism and communist involvement had been, in effect, purged from collective memory. AFSCME and teachers' unions had begun as lobbying agencies, and in recent years met with the legislature's Joint Finance Committee year to year. With their political allies, the unions had then presented budget details to the governor for signature. To undertake a dramatically more militant approach, serious preparation for a different scale of events and mobilization would have been mandatory. Other than a call for members to come to protest actions and take part in recall efforts, the effort had not been made.

As the weeks after the last-minute mobilization in mid-June prompted labor and other activists to public contemplation—largely by way of tweeting and retweeting—the narrative of "life-changing experience" loomed large. Something, for thousands of participants, had happened that would remain a foundation for a different life, or at least a different way of looking at their own public and private lives. Republicans gloated that they had withstood the best that their opponents had to offer. Protesters saw it the other way around: they had found each other as they came to understand what was being taken away and, more important, came to understand those who joined them from across all sorts of previous barriers.

As the new laws took effect, deadening so many aspects of Wisconsin life, one question that remained was whether the labor solidarity of the spring was a sort of go-down-with-your-boots-on heroism or marked the possibility of a new beginning. But this could not be the only question, because the share of organized labor within the public sphere had been redefined as the public sphere itself became better understood—and not only by union members and retirees.

FURTHER READING

Holter, Darryl, ed., *Workers and Unions in Wisconsin: A Labor History Anthology*, Madison: State Historical Society of Wisconsin, 1999.

Ozanne, Robert, *The Labor Movement in Wisconsin: A History*, Madison: State Historical Society of Wisconsin, 1984.

SOLIDARITY 1970

STORY BY **PAUL BUHLE**

ART BY **GARY DUMM**

...WE ARE EMPLOYEES, NOT STUDENTS, IN OUR ROLE AS T.A.S WE TEACH 30% OF THE CLASS CONTACT HOURS.

WHAT WE **WANT** IS A **FOUR** YEAR APPOINTMENT, **NOT** SEMESTER-TO-SEMESTER HIRING, WE WANT **OUR** WORKLOAD TO BE 20 HOURS FOR **HALF-TIME** WORK.

WE WANT A GRIEVANCE PROCEDURE **INDEPENDENT** OF FACULTY **CONTROL**, AND AN INDEPENDENT ARBITRATOR. WE WANT **DECISIONS** TO BE MADE **EQUALLY** BY FACULTY, STUDENTS AND T.A.S, NOT BY FACULTY-ADMINISTRATION **TOP-DOWN** CONTROL.

WHY WOULD YOU **MAKE** ALL OF THESE **DEMANDS?**

WE ARE ALL ON THE **SAME SIDE**, AND YOU'LL BE **PROFESSORS** SOME DAY!

LATER...

WE HAVE **NO CHOICE** BUT TO **STRIKE.**

IT WON'T BE **EASY.** SUPPORT FROM THE **LABOR** MOVEMENT WOULD HELP A **LOT**, NO MATTER **HOW** WELL **STUDENTS** SUPPORT US.

AND STUDENTS DO STEP UP...

SUPPORT THE STRIKE

SUPPORT THE STRIKE

SUPPORT THE STRIKE

12 A WISCONSIN TEACHER'S SUICIDE

By Matthew Rothschild

Jeri-Lynn Betts, an early childhood teacher in the Watertown, Wisconsin, school district, died on March 8, an apparent suicide.

A colleague says she was "very distraught" because of Governor Scott Walker's attacks on public-sector workers and public education.

Betts, fifty-six, was a dedicated teacher who was admired in the Watertown community.

"She was an amazing person," says the Reverend Terry Larson of the Immanuel Evangelical Lutheran Church in Watertown, where she was a member. "She really put her heart and soul in her work." Larson officiated at her memorial service on March 15.

"She was one of the good guys," says Karen Stefonek, who used to teach with Betts. "She was very, very dedicated and worked so well with the little special needs children. She just was very, very good with them and very well respected in the district."

In the days after Betts's death, two members of the school district contacted the *Progressive* about her death, calling it a suicide and saying it was connected, at least in part, to the policies that Walker had proposed. He was demanding that public workers, including teachers, contribute a significant amount of their salaries to health care and pensions. And in his budget he proposed taking $900 million out of the public schools, imposing a freeze on property taxes so local governments couldn't chip in more for education, and allowing any student, regardless of income, to go to a private school with a taxpayer subsidy.

"She was definitely very distraught about it," said one of her coworkers, who requested anonymity. "She was feeling a lot of stress about the legislation that was going through."

"She was concerned about the cuts teachers would have to take," said another, who also requested anonymity. This coworker added that Betts's colleagues acknowledged her anguish about the governor's policies in their discussions after her death.

Figuring out all the contributing factors behind a likely suicide is a complicated problem. Such deaths are in some ways incomprehensible—and always tragic.

But the report from the Watertown police gives some clues. A police officer took a statement from Susan Kemmerling, who worked with Betts as a special education paraprofessional for the past decade.

"Susan advised me that Geri [sic] had a long history of depression," Officer Jeffrey Meloy wrote in his report. "Susan stated that the last several weeks had been 'stressing her [Betts] out' due to the protests and the introduction of the budget repair bill and the uncertainty involved in the teaching world, as far as who was going to have jobs and what services were going to be cut ... Susan stated that Jeri truly loved her job and was about the most outgoing and bubbly person you could ever want to be around. Susan stated that everybody had noticed, however, the last few weeks since the introduction of the budget repair bill that Jeri was having a lot of difficulty." Meloy also interviewed Bonnie Lauersdorf, a physical therapist who worked with Betts for the past twenty-five years and had been a friend of hers "for most of her adult life," the report says. She told the officer that Jeri was concerned about "the uncertainty of what the budget was going to do to her retirement" and about "cuts to the school districts and possible cuts to the special ed program." Lauersdorf added that "Jeri felt like she was being 'forced out,' " the report says.

Walker's policies are placing a heavy strain on teachers, according to Steve Cupery, the director of the Lakewood UniServ Council, the teachers' union in Watertown.

"There's a lot of stress, especially among older teachers," he says. "They're concerned about being targeted. And there's the stress associated with the potential loss of benefits, which could amount to a substantial cut in pay."

Cupery adds that teachers are worried that class sizes will grow, workloads will increase, and that they will not be able to "develop curriculum material around the individual needs of students."

Walker's policies have "shredded the morale of teachers," said Wisconsin state assemblywoman Sondy Pope-Roberts on March 16. "The cuts to school districts are going to be drastic."

Pat Theder, Jefferson County coroner, looked into Betts's death. "Our investigation is still pending," he said. "We're waiting for a toxicology report. She may have ingested something. We're doing toxicology to determine if she took over the therapeutic amount of her medication and whether that was enough to kill her." This theory was later confirmed.

Betts's old colleague Karen Stefonek remembers her as fun-loving and as someone who loved to travel.

Her death "took a lot out of us," Stefonek says. "It hit us in the heart."

AFTERWORD

This was one of the tougher stories I've ever written, and it has stayed with me now for months.

It was tough mostly because, as I found out more about Jeri-Lynn Betts, I came to admire and sympathize with her. She struggled with depression much of her adult life, and depression can be an enormous weight. According to friends, she was handling her depression well, and had been for years, until Governor Walker's assault on collective bargaining and public education.

She was an extremely conscientious early childhood teacher. She was worried about what would happen to her program if the legislature approved Walker's cuts. She was concerned that she was being forced into early retirement, and she was distressed about whether she would have enough to live on.

By all accounts, her students meant everything to her. So much so that, on the morning she committed suicide, she sent an email to the school to make sure someone would check on one of her students who had head lice. That particular detail still hits me hard, though for some reason I didn't include it in the original piece.

The story was also tough because it was so tricky to report. Though I was tipped off by two employees of the school district where she worked, they wouldn't speak on the record. When I called the superintendent, he flat-out lied to me and said her death had nothing to do with Walker and that I was "way off base." He then ordered all employees of the school district not to speak with me.

I called more than thirty colleagues of Jeri-Lynn Betts at home, and no one would talk. Many hung up right away. A few got angry. Only when I demanded to see a copy of the police report was I able to piece everything together.

For me, the moral of the story is Scott Walker's callousness. Yes, Jeri-Lynn Betts may have been psychologically fragile. But Walker's policies pushed her over the edge. He is inflicting great economic and psychological pain on many, many public-sector workers.

But he doesn't care. He still acts like he's just playing some political game, having fun roughhousing on the ideological playground and carrying water for the Koch brothers. But in reality he's messing with people's lives here. It's a crying shame.

WALKERCARE

13 THE ROLE OF CORPORATIONS

By Roger Bybee

The first few months of Wisconsin Governor Scott Walker's regime have brazenly signaled a policy of disinvestment in public education, health care, and the environment and an assault on worker rights, that is, the dismantling of proud elements of the state's uniquely reform-minded history.

Walker's disinvestment in the public sector parallels the disinvestment by major corporations in Wisconsin's productive base since the early 1970s, with huge firms shifting capital away from modernization of their factories to speculation on Wall Street and uprooting family-supporting jobs from Wisconsin communities and transplanting them to low-wage, high-repression nations like Mexico and China. This intensifying pattern of disinvestment and offshoring shows decisively how thoroughly corporations in Wisconsin and elsewhere have repudiated the social contract that once prevailed between labor and capital, when unions achieved recognition and relatively high wages and benefits, while management was assured of labor discipline and an affluent base of domestic consumers.

Just as Walker's contemptuous renunciation of public workers' rights (a mere "expensive entitlement") and public investment in shared institutions triggered a massive uprising led by labor in 2011, the abandonment of workers and communities by Wisconsin corporations has been igniting battles in the streets of Wisconsin's factory towns for four decades. Starting in the 1970s, when the corporate exodus began, and flaring up episodically as the offshoring of jobs accelerated, industrial unions and their allies have persistently challenged the once-sacrosanct right of private corporations to invest wherever they choose and asserted the radical notion that workers and communities have a claim to corporate resources.

Coalitions of industrial unions and community groups, often ad hoc, occasionally achieved their goal, forcing corporations to reverse their plans to flee the state, but most often the coalitions failed. But they have nonetheless made clear to a broad audience the essential conflict between economic security for local workers and the fundamental imperative of capitalism: maximum profits. These movements forcefully challenged the comfortable notion that maximum corporate profits could be equated with the well-being of the entire community and nation, a notion that has gained increasing credibility among elites even as the nation grows profoundly more unequal.

The fight by Wisconsin's industrial unions, especially those concentrated in the southeast corner of Milwaukee, Racine, and Kenosha, against plant closings and investor-rights agreements like the North American Free Trade Agreement (NAFTA), contributed an important stream of anticorporate rebellion to the mighty river that converged in Madison in February–March 2011.

ONCE A PROMISED LAND

Before the struggles over job retention and public influence on corporate investments in recent years, Wisconsin was a mecca for people willing to work hard in grueling industrial jobs to support their families. For example, my maternal grandfather, an unemployed industrial worker in St. Louis, brought his family 350 miles north to the promised land of southeastern Wisconsin in a crowded railroad boxcar. It was about 1917, when my mother was three or four.

Wisconsin offered plenty of factory jobs, and my grandfather, who was a Socialist, eventually found a niche on the assembly line at the American Motors plant in Kenosha. He worked there for more than thirty years and was a proud member of United Auto Workers Local 72, which had been formed to control the brutal pace of the assembly line and to gain a decent standard of living. My other grandfather, born in Illinois, wandered the Midwest as a hotel bellboy and semipro baseball player before settling in Racine. But his outspoken role as a union advocate and Socialist got him fired three times. Nonetheless, industrial unionism, led by the Congress of Industrial Organizations, spread like a prairie fire across Wisconsin. For example, Racine industry was 85 percent unionized by 1937, according to a study of Wisconsin by the Work Projects Administration. The Depression years were also accompanied by the election of several Socialist mayors in the state.

The auto industry (which once employed 38,000 workers), farm equipment factories, rubber works, leather goods factories, and other operations produced a vast stream of products and attracted eager workers from throughout the nation to southeastern Wisconsin in particular. The rapid unionization of the region in the 1930s became a foundation of working-class prosperity and power, producing excellent wages and benefits that allowed thousands of workers to send their children to college, secure a stable retirement, and develop a strong voice inside the plant and in Wisconsin politics.

The state's stable industrial base began to erode in the late 1960s and early 1970s as some Wisconsin employers, such as Howard Industries and Ouster of Racine, and Square D and Cutler Hammer in Milwaukee, to name but a few, started to shift jobs to the low-wage, antiunion South, where "right-to-work" laws made it possible for management to selectively hire antiunion workers and block any union beachheads.

During the 1970s and since, the class consciousness that had existed for generations among industrial workers would explode periodically as workers protested in the streets against local plant closings, fought for legislation providing workers with protections against the impact of shutdowns, and waged extensive battles against free-trade agreements that accelerated the flight of jobs to Mexico and China and, worse, provided their disappearance with a government seal of approval.

Industrial unions such as the United Auto Workers, International Association of Machinists, United Electrical Radio and Machine Workers, United Steelworkers, and Allied Industrial Workers (later to merge with the steelworkers), among others, engaged in numerous local fights to preserve jobs. A constant theme was the radical notion that working people and communities had a right to participate in decisions about their workplaces. This of course conflicted with both the long-held basic "right" of capitalists to make private investments unilaterally and with the free-market fundamentalism increasingly championed by corporate, political, and media elites. The industrial unions insisted that the future of workers, their jobs, and their communities should not be left up to the whims of distant CEOs.

Industrial workers also fought corporations' use of federal and state subsidies to transfer jobs, insisting that taxpayer dollars should be used to foster the growth of family-supporting jobs rather than their degradation into subsistence-level work in the US South or abroad.

The largest mobilizations involving corporate disinvestment were conducted against NAFTA, with numerous actions occurring across the state, and against the World Trade Organization, when in 1999 hundreds of Wisconsin trade unionists took part in the "Battle of Seattle," where the WTO sought to convene. Union members, retirees, and other activists continue to battle against upcoming free-trade agreements, like those with South Korea, Colombia (the world's consistent leader in assassinations of trade union leaders), and Panama championed by the Obama administration. While some observers attribute Barack Obama's critical Wisconsin primary victory in February 2008 to his memorable speeches in opposition to free-trade agreements on his way to the presidency, Obama soon began actively promoting NAFTA-style agreements in the name of job creation.

The movements against unilateral corporate investment faced not only double-talking Democrats but an elite consensus in Wisconsin about the importance of developing the best possible "business climate," and a similarly strong faith among corporate, political, and media leaders that corporate globalization would strengthen Wisconsin's economy.

These movements were faced with internal difficulties as well. Those choosing to confront corporations about their decisions to leave Wisconsin often found that leaders of their own unions harbored the illusion that further concessions could persuade the CEOs to maintain jobs in Wisconsin rather than pocket the workers' givebacks and merely delay the relocation for a couple years. Insurgent workers often found themselves dealing with union officials who viewed their role as veritable funeral directors, negotiating orderly plant-closing and severance agreements and avoiding the unfamiliar terrain of mobilizing members, developing allies among other unions and community groups, and pressuring Democratic allies to do more than line up training funds for the victims of the shutdown. Conducting effective campaigns against disinvestment policies of corporations and the government has required some key institutional bases to ignite and sustain these fights.

After looking at the "business climate" consensus that isolated unions from many of their traditional liberal and Democratic allies,

I will discuss the effects of corporate disinvestment on Wisconsin's productive base, deconstruct Scott Walker's strategy to divide private- and public-sector workers, and then look at some of the more notable battles about disinvestment.

BUSINESS CLIMATE SET AS STATE'S KEY GOAL

Employer flight provided corporate elites with an opportunity to gain leverage over public policy with the assertion that Wisconsin's attainment of a "good business climate" relative to other states would be good for all Wisconsin citizens.

In 1973 the *Milwaukee Journal*, then one of the nation's leading liberal newspapers, published a relentless stream of front-page articles by a University of Wisconsin business professor—his work financed by a corporate-funded think tank—arguing that Wisconsin needed to lower its corporate taxes to remain competitive. The immediate result of pressure from Wisconsin Manufacturers and Commerce and the *Journal* was a property-tax exemption for machinery and equipment, enacted under Democratic governor Patrick Lucey and ardently supported by future Democratic governor Anthony Earl, then a legislative leader. (The Journal Company itself benefited handsomely from the exemption.)

Because taxes are a relatively trivial consideration in business location decisions, the exemption for machinery and equipment failed to magnetically attract firms from other states or even to prevent Wisconsin manufacturing firms from first fully exploiting the tax break and then relocating to the low-wage South, Mexico, or overseas. Briggs & Stratton, for example, gained an estimated $50 million in savings as it downsized its Milwaukee manufacturing operations from about 9,000 to 2,000 workers, with the work relocated to low-wage Mexico, China, and sites in the US Sun Belt. Joe Chambers, an officer of Allied Industrial Workers Local 232, noted that the workers had given substantial concessions to Briggs during the preceding decade (roughly 1983–93). Even after earning record profits in 1993, Briggs moved an additional 2,000 jobs out of Milwaukee in search of ever-greater record profits.

The lesson drawn by political and media elites from the continued flight of industry was not that tax breaks were a futile method of retaining jobs and allowed corporations to essentially take the money and run. Even considering such a conclusion would have opened public debate about such questions as how to establish an effective public role in heretofore private decisions made by corporations when those decisions have a broad and devastating social impact. Such public debate is commonplace in Europe. It also would have added support to the call for the adoption of an industrial policy in the United States that would have asserted a substantial role for the federal government in preventing plant closings, ensuring balanced regional development, and providing decent incomes and economic security to workers.

A very different conclusion came to monopolize public discourse in Wisconsin. Corporate leaders and both Democratic and Republican elites interpreted each shift of jobs out of Wisconsin as a warning signal that the state needed to make its "business climate" still more comfortable for business leaders. This conclusion was reinforced by news coverage and editorials throughout the state's dominant media, without any reference to actual data that documented Wisconsin's status as one of the nation's lower-taxed states for business.

The constant effort to perfect the business climate became the overriding goal of both Democratic and Republican administrations since the 1970s. As a result, more than 60 percent of Wisconsin firms with more than $100 million in revenue pay no corporate state income taxes, at a time when state's manufacturing base is severely depleted. Ernst & Young, the respected accounting firm, calculated in April that Wisconsin offered brand-new corporations the fourth-lowest corporate taxes in the nation.

The dominance of the "business climate" paradigm made Republicans aggressive, allowing them to brand every tax or regulation of corporations as a "barrier to jobs," as if full employment, rather than greater profits for their corporate campaign contributors, were their primary aim. Having swallowed the fundamental GOP assumptions—that public policy might affect corporate decision making about the location of new plants and that proposed state policies must pass muster with corporate leaders before adoption—Democrats allowed themselves to be placed on the defensive.

The administrations of Democratic governors since Patrick Lucey have been consumed with concerns about the so-called business climate and relations with business leaders, with Governor Anthony Earl (1983–86) memorably cutting both unemployment compensation benefits and taxes on the wealthy. When acceptable policy is defined as policy that has corporate approval, even the most progressive members of the legislature, along with the state employee unions, predictably fail to stress that lower corporate taxes do not produce more jobs in Wisconsin and that Wisconsin actually imposes a relatively light tax burden on corporations.

In recent decades the basic outcome of this uncritical worship of the business climate has been a steady decline in the share of taxes borne by Wisconsin businesses and a commensurate rise in property taxes and fees borne by ordinary citizens, such as the University of Wisconsin's soaring tuition.

Beginning in the late 1980s and early 1990s, the primacy of the business climate was augmented by arguments about keeping up with "global competition"—and the way to remain competitive was defined as wringing wage concessions from workers, and gaining tax cuts and regulatory changes for corporations at both the state and federal levels. The *Milwaukee Journal* ran a series on adapting to the world economy that encouraged unions to recognize the presumed unalterable reality of globalization and passively "get used to it." The series also advised that plant closings and relocations of "low-value" jobs should be accepted in exchange for the certainty of gaining the higher-skilled, higher-paying jobs that would surely follow passage of measures like NAFTA.

Yet even with all the efforts to appease corporate decision-makers, the outflow of industrial jobs to low-wage nations has accelerated. Retraining programs failed to help the vast majority of dislocated workers find family-supporting jobs, as the availability of such employment continues to dry up even for workers with enhanced skills. The offshoring phenomenon spread even to professional jobs. Alan Blinder, a Princeton professor, estimated that 38 million to 42 million professional jobs in the United States were "highly off-shorable." In contrast to job growth of 20 percent to 38 percent in every decade since 1940, corporate America generated close to zero job growth in the two decades between 1990 and 2009.

Corporate investment choices—such as GM's closing its 2,800-worker plant in Janesville, Wisconsin; Chrysler's use of Obama administration–provided bailout funds to shift the last 850 auto jobs in Wisconsin to Mexico; and a hedge fund's decision to close Wisconsin's most technologically advanced plant in Kimberly—left behind industrial communities that are mere shells. These cities have little realistic prospect for a return to prosperity under the prevailing market-guided strategies favored by the Democratic Obama administration, whose formulas for local recovery mirror those pushed by the George W. Bush administration.

DISINVESTMENT IN THE PRODUCTIVE BASE

Despite the enshrinement of the business climate as Wisconsin's driving purpose, the state has experienced a disappearance of unionized jobs that provided working-class people with a nearly middle-class standard of living. The toll of corporate disinvestment was evident in industrial cities across Wisconsin. Milwaukee, for example, was once known as the Machine Tool Capital of the World. But between 1977 and today, Milwaukee has lost fully 80 percent of its manufacturing jobs, according to Marc Levine, an urban economist at UW–Milwaukee. Homegrown industrial giants have shed thousands of jobs, with firms like A. O. Smith (now Tower Automotive), Master Lock (now part of American Brands), and Johnson Controls transferring more jobs to Mexico than they had in Milwaukee. Johnson Controls, already operating thirty plants in China, is opening ten more. Allen-Bradley, now part of Rockwell, once employed 5,500 production workers belonging to the United Electrical Radio and Machine Workers. It now employs none locally but has extensive production facilities in China and Mexico and other low-wage sites. The economist Jeff Faux has estimated that manufacturing wage rates in China average about 3 percent of those in the United States, while in Mexico the figure is 10 percent.

The consequences of this disinvestment have been sweeping and catastrophic. A huge chunk of the blue-collar middle class has fallen into the ranks of the working poor. Milwaukee is now the fourth-poorest major city in the nation. Nine of ten inner-city hospitals have closed, and infant mortality rates in Milwaukee's central city, where the population is primarily African American and Latino, are at levels usually seen in some of the poorest underdeveloped countries. The African American working class, long the target of virulent discrimination, nonetheless managed to produce family incomes 19 percent above the national average, thanks to the once-plentiful supply of unionized jobs that provided good pay and protections against bias. As of 2006, the average black family income had fallen to 23 percent below the national average. UW–Milwaukee researchers Marc Levine and R. L. McNeely, in separate studies, have concluded that the social infrastructure has now been destroyed by deindustrialization and that 50 percent to 63 percent of African American males are unemployed or discouraged workers. At the same time, Wisconsin now has the second-highest rate of incarceration among black males in the nation, and its overall prison population has climbed about eightfold since 1970, from 2,973 to 23,112 at the end of 2009, good evidence of the consequence of joblessness.

In my hometown of Racine, new jails and prisons seem to be the principal growth industry, whereas the city has lost more than 13,500 factory jobs since 1979. The county recently completed a $30 million jail with six times the capacity of the one completed in 1980. A juvenile corrections facility now sits, symptomatically, where the Rainfair clothing factory stood before its new owners sent the jobs to China. The destruction of human potential reaches into virtually all of Wisconsin's industrial cities, affecting health, family stability, increases in both family and street violence, children's performance in school, falling home values representing the life savings of most families, the rising rate of home foreclosures, and a host of other indicators of distress.

In Wausau, a central Wisconsin industrial city of 38,000 where the unemployment rate was higher than 14 percent in 2010, jobless and underemployed workers make drastic improvisations to survive. "Every week we run into people who try to pull their own teeth," said Laura Scudiere, executive director of the Bridge Clinic in Wausau. "It's like a third world country when it comes to dental health." In Janesville, a southeastern Wisconsin city of 55,000, the December 2008 closing of the General Motors plant meant the loss of 2,800 jobs at GM and about 3,000 at suppliers. The shutdown was followed within three months by a near-tripling of the number of battered women seeking shelter in the city.

With Wisconsin's manufacturing unions grievously weakened, corporate vultures swooped in to drive down wages, reduce benefits, and weaken workers' rights to effective representation. Mercury Marine, located in Fond du Lac, insisted its workers accept a lengthy list of painful concessions—most notably, the imposition of a permanent two-tier wage structure that will lower base pay over time. Mercury Marine used the threat of shifting all its 1,500 jobs to Oklahoma if members of the International Association of Machinists refused the concessions.

Harley-Davidson workers in Milwaukee, members of the United Steelworkers and the International Association of Machinists, were next. Workers there were also threatened with relocation of their jobs unless they accepted a permanent reduction of the workforce and a multitier pay structure that will push down wages. Adding insult to injury, Harley officials who had accompanied President Obama to the Far East announced a few months later that they were opening a new low-wage factory in India.

With the precedents of Mercury Marine and Harley much discussed in the media, United Auto Workers Local 833 prepared for similar demands from the Kohler Corporation, which is located near Sheboygan. A militant local that successfully waged the longest strike in US history, the UAW started its negotiations with an impressive rally of 3,000 members and community supporters in opposition to concessions. But once negotiations got rolling, the UAW soon found itself with a gun pointed at its head: swallow massive concessions—including a multitier wage structure that would degrade pay and benefits, and vastly increased health-care payments for retirees—or watch their jobs being sent overseas, where more than half of Kohler's workers live.

FIGHTING CORPORATE DISINVESTMENT

Occasional low-profile fights against corporate shutdowns in Wisconsin occurred during the 1970s but failed to capture the imagination of either union leaders or the general public. The United Electrical Radio and Machine Workers Local 1111 tried valiantly to build a permanent coalition to challenge the rising tide of job loss but was unable to persuade some key major unions to join the fight.

In 1982, as unemployment in Racine began to soar toward Great Depression levels, McGraw-Edison, a division of Cooper Industries, announced that it intended to shut down its Racine lighting plant, a profitable, modern facility. The Citizen/Labor Coalition to Save Jobs was formed, drawing in a variety of labor organizations, religious leaders (the Dominican sisters were a particularly active group), and community groups. At news conferences and on the front pages of the weekly *Racine Labor*, the coalition continually stressed the astronomical pay of McGraw's CEO (by 1982 standards) of $900,000 and the corporation's 56 percent increase in profits in the previous year.

Workers' efforts climaxed in a march from a nearby church to the plant and a rally of 500 that received extensive media coverage. Company officials complained bitterly to union leaders about the way that McGraw was being mercilessly "beaten up" by *Racine Labor* and other media outlets, and McGraw relented within a few days of the march. It would remain in Racine, but only if workers accepted a 10 percent pay cut that seemed to many observers as exacting a purely symbolic pound of flesh in exchange for keeping the plant open. The primarily female workforce had an average income of $14,000 a year and deeply resented the pay cut, but workers eventually voted to accept it.

With a sense of pride from their victory in saving their jobs, and a determination that workers should have the last word, a delegation of UAW Local 1877 members made a dramatic surprise appearance at the corporate stockholders' meeting in Chicago a few weeks later. Quickly brushing past security guards, the UAW members distributed flyers to the stunned stockholders. The leaflets called upon McGraw-Edison to renounce the use of blackmail tactics to exploit the fears of working people, to issue a "policy on plant closings that will insure that the needs of affected workers, family members, and communities are considered," and to provide workers and communities with a formal mechanism for participating in corporate investment decisions.

Although hardly an unalloyed victory, the McGraw-Edison experience in Racine showed the sixty union locals there, and the hundreds more in southeastern Wisconsin, that fighting back against threatened plant closings could produce unexpected results. It also illustrated the importance of union leadership's becoming united in fighting the shutdown and the value of labor-owned media in publicizing the struggle (with a circulation of nearly 17,000 in a city of about 80,000, *Racine Labor* had extensive reach and impact).

In the fall of 1982, as joblessness in Racine kept climbing (reaching 19.9 percent in December), the Canada-based Massey-Ferguson, maker of farm equipment, announced that it would be closing its Racine warehouse and shifting the work to Iowa. The 200 members of United Auto Workers Local 244 (I was briefly a member) who worked at the plant were outraged at the announcement because they had twice given concessions, totaling about $4 an hour, based on explicit pledges that Massey would keep the Racine warehouse open.

The Citizen/Labor Coalition to Save Jobs again sprang to life and began formulating plans to build a broader coalition to fight the Massey shutdown. Meanwhile, the bargaining committee of the International Association of Machinists (IAM), in negotiations with Interlake Manufacturing, was stunned to learn that the corporation had planned to close the plant and move the jobs to Charleston, South Carolina. However, a company executive informed the IAM, Interlake officials had seen the public pressure applied to Massey-Ferguson and had concluded, "We saw what you guys were doing to Massey, and we didn't want to be put through that."

On December 2, 1982, Racine's rapidly deteriorating jobs crisis, coupled with an unseasonably warm day, produced a march and rally of 800 to 1,000 people from area unions, progressive organizations, faith groups, and civil rights and antipoverty groups on Racine's north side, the site of numerous closed factories. A high-energy rally held at the packed Racine Labor Center featured denunciations of Massey, corporate America, and Ronald Reagan for policies that betrayed working people and communities and then freely abandoned them in search of cheaper labor, depriving them of the means to survive.

When the UAW resumed negotiations with Massey the following Monday, the corporate representatives announced that the warehouse was staying in Racine. Once again, a high-profile publicity campaign and massive show of community support for the workers had prevailed, showing the community that corporations have an obligation to workers and communities as well as shareholders.

In 1984 Massey-Ferguson again prepared to close down the Racine operation by lining up a $5.8 million federal Urban Development Action Grant. Again, Local 244 and the local coalition went to work, this time aided by the late Democratic representative Les Aspin. Although a hawkish supporter of Reagan's foreign policies, Aspin recognized his self-interest in preserving jobs when Racine was still consistently among the cities with the highest unemployment. Aspin helped to promote a petition drive that gathered 11,000 signatures, and other local public officials denounced the proposed use of taxpayer dollars to rob one depressed community of jobs and shift them to another city. In the end, Republican backers of the grant had to back down, and the jobs at Massey were saved once more.

Following these efforts, a group of progressive labor leaders began to join together around the editorial board of *Racine Labor*. One product of this group was a full-page ad that ran in late 1987 in *Racine Labor* calling upon Aspin to oppose US aid to the murderous Nicaraguan contras, whom he previously had supported, and to support initiatives toward peace and autonomy. The letter described the goal of US policy in Central America as "making Mexico and Central America safe for runaway shops." It was signed by sixty-nine Wisconsin labor leaders, many of whom resisted pressure from top union officials to remain silent.

Many of those same leaders also went to work in early 1988 when Chrysler CEO Lee Iacocca broke his pledges to United Auto Workers Local 72 and state and local governments by announcing the shutdown of auto production in Kenosha, which would eliminate 5,500 jobs. The shutdown was part of a three-cornered move, whereby the Kenosha jobs were being sent to Detroit, Detroit jobs were being shifted to Mexico, and Kenosha would be left with just 1,200 engine production jobs.

Led by the articulate and witty shop chair Rudy Kuzel, Local 72 unified behind a comprehensive plan to build a wide coalition to resist the shutdown every step of the way. The union's first move was to invite the Reverend Jesse Jackson, then running for the Democratic presidential nomination, to address a rally. The rally drew 8,000 to 10,000 members of Local 72 and their supporters, and all Milwaukee TV stations broadcast the event live. Jackson denounced "the economic violence" of Chrysler's decision, arguing that it would lead to the decimation of the community. All of Wisconsin's political leadership—including the conservative Republican governor Tommy Thompson—agreed to threaten Chrysler with a lawsuit unless it retained the jobs in Kenosha.

Despite opposition from top UAW leaders, Local 72 endorsed Jackson in the presidential primary and maintained a high local and national profile with rallies, news conferences, and a congressional hearing in Washington, DC, at which I testified. Preventing the Chrysler shutdown became such a central issue that Al Gore, then the Democrats' most conservative presidential contender, favoring aid to the contras and free-market economics, suddenly reversed field and ran a TV ad that ended with the tagline "Al Gore: People before profits."

Eventually, Thompson and Aspin backed off suing Chrysler, and UAW Local 72 was left standing alone, bereft of support from public officials, although it maintained labor's backing. Ultimately, Chrysler killed the 5,500 auto-production jobs in Racine, but Local 72 succeeded in pressuring Chrysler into the most expensive plant-closing agreement (covering pensions, severance, retraining, health care, and other benefits) that had been granted up to that point.

During the 1990s five iconic Milwaukee employers—A. O. Smith, Master Lock, Johnson Controls, Rockwell Automotive (formerly Allen-Bradley), and Briggs & Stratton—relocated vast numbers of jobs. Union officials at A. O. Smith and Master Lock seemingly were unable to persuade their members that the huge loss of jobs to Mexico could be prevented. The influence of the prevailing ideology—that corporate globalization is inevitable and cannot be stopped—apparently had a major effect in those two instances.

On a Friday night in October 1996, Johnson Controls provided veteran workers at a valve plant employing 180 with prizes for their years of service. On the following Tuesday the corporation conveyed its true sense of how much the workers were valued: officials told IAM members that their jobs were being sent to Mexico, where the workers would receive about 72 cents an hour. While IAM's leadership at the plant was eager to hold a news conference with the pro-labor filmmaker Michael Moore the following day to denounce the corporation's treatment of workers, a top local official canceled the event so that he could negotiate to save the jobs. No protest took place, no job-saving agreement was reached, and the jobs went to Mexico anyway.

Briggs & Stratton's aggressive cuts in jobs and their impact on the Milwaukee community were severely underplayed by the *Milwaukee Journal Sentinel*, although it had a team of perceptive business reporters covering the firm. (They were persistently criticized by company officials, and all eventually wound up leaving the Briggs beat.) Briggs CEO Fred Stratton was treated to a front-page, softball interview in the *Journal Sentinel*, while *Milwaukee Magazine*—an upper-middle-class lifestyle publication—also defended Stratton in a cover story. Meanwhile, the union was riven by left–right political splits and, from my perspective, tended to emphasize an in-plant strategy to lower production and a campaign to pressure corporate board members, at the expense of more community outreach through Milwaukee's 200 union locals and hundreds of religious congregations. The union also lost a libel lawsuit to the litigious corporation and increasingly lost leverage as more jobs were moved out. At Rockwell, UE Local 1111 tried a variety of tactics at both the bargaining table and with street rallies. With its membership declining and the lack of a unified citywide or regional movement of labor and community groups to preserve jobs and challenge capital's right to relocate jobs from an already-impoverished city, Local 1111 found itself unable to halt Rockwell's flight. But the UE's nonstop efforts allowed it to succeed in negotiating work for almost every member until they had a chance to retire, up to the end of 2010.

During the summer of 2008 the 600 long-time workers at the Kimberly Paper plant in the tiny town of Kimberly (population: 2,500) were stunned to learn that the plant's new owners were closing the plant despite its profitability and its highly advanced technology. The new owner was a paper-making conglomerate called NewPage, which in turn is owned by a powerful New York private equity fund called Cerberus, whose leading figures include John Snow, commerce secretary in the second Bush administration; former vice president Dan Quayle; and Stephen Feinberg, the reclusive founder of Cerberus who alone was paid $15 million in 2008. With the Kimberly plant, Cerberus was practicing the common tactic of asset stripping. As the labor expert Stephen Lerner explained, "The buyout business remains, at its core, a vehicle for the spectacular accumulation of wealth by the few, without regard for the impact on others."

In September 2008, members of United Steelworkers Local 2-9 and their diverse set of community supporters—town officials, US Representative Steve Kagen, local ministers, small businesspeople—held a rally of 5,000 calling upon Cerberus to run the plant or sell it to one of the four companies interested in buying it. But even with congressional pressure, Cerberus remained unmoved, and the plant stood empty nearly three years later.

The struggles recounted here—to save family-supporting jobs and contest what capital regards as its unilateral right to discard workers and communities—often ended in failure. But the battles waged by industrial unions and their allies, overcoming internal opposition and uniform hostility or disinterest from corporate, political, and media elites, have helped countless Wisconsinites to fully understand the uncompromising determination of the global investor class to drive down wages, destroy valued public institutions, and usurp democracy itself. As a result, the fights waged by Wisconsin's industrial unions contributed immensely to illuminating how and where Scott Walker intends to drag Wisconsin in the global race to the bottom.

AFTERWORD: LABOR DAY IN WISCONSIN

Labor Day 2011 was marked by high spirits and huge crowds in Wisconsin. In Madison, guitarist Tom Morello (of the band Rage Against the Machine) was welcomed back for a high-powered concert where he displayed the same spirit of solidarity that brought him to the city earlier this year.

Morello, who plays solo under the name The Nightwatchman, was incongruously honored with a bagpipe salute from the International Association of Firefighters Local 311, a greeting that was emblematic of the kind of merging of diverse cultural and political styles that has kept the ongoing Wisconsin Rebellion rolling.

In Wausau, workers heartily booed anti-worker US Representative Sean Duffy and State Senator Pam Galloway, both Republican Tea Party supporters, when they appeared at the Labor Day parade in this hard-hit central Wisconsin city. And in Milwaukee, the annual Labor Fest along the shore of Lake Michigan was even more packed than usual, with members of different unions clad in a rainbow of t-shirts emblazoned with their union logo and a message of solidarity.

Along with the huge contingents of unionists, a mélange of progressive cultural projects put on a dazzling display of activity from the city's multiracial youth: young Latinos and Latinas in feathered Mayan costumes dancing along the street, giant puppets depicting corporate greed and civil rights and labor heroes, and colorful floats with pro-labor messages.

But a keen awareness of labor's plight nationally and in Wisconsin was never far from the minds of those attending. People with clipboards were surrounded by unionists eager to sign petitions calling for the recall of Scott Walker, the driving force behind the state's new virtual ban on public-employee unionism.

FURTHER READING

Piven, Frances Fox and Richard Cloward, *The Breaking of the American Social Contract*, New York: The New Press, 1998.

Hacker, Jacob S. and Paul Pierson, *Winner Take-All Politics: How Washington Made the Rich Richer—and Turned Its Back on the Middle Class*, New York: Simon & Schuster, 2010.

Faux, Jeff, *The Global Class War: How America's Bi-Partisan Elite Lost Our Future and What It Will Take to Win It Back*, Hoboken, NJ: John Wiley & Sons, 2006.

© SHARON RUDAHL 2011

Part 5 BEYOND WISCONSIN

15 WISCONSIN AND US LABOR

By Kim Scipes

As people mobilized in Madison to oppose Governor Scott Walker's attack on public-sector unions and collective bargaining, his actions touched a nerve among working people across the country and stimulated workers to again assert themselves without apology.

By February 20 rallies had begun taking place, and by mid-March they would be held in cities as divergent as (in alphabetical order) Albany, New York; Atlanta; Austin; Baltimore; Boise, Idaho; Boston; Chicago; Columbus, Ohio; Corpus Christi, Texas; Denver; Des Moines; Harrisburg, Pennsylvania; Helena, Montana; Indianapolis; Jefferson City, Missouri; Lansing, Michigan; Little Rock, Arkansas; Miami; Minneapolis; Nashville; New York City; Oakland, California; Olympia, Washington; Philadelphia; Richmond, Virginia; Sacramento; San Diego; San Jose, California; San Francisco; Santa Fe; Seattle; Springfield, Illinois; St. Paul, Minnesota; Tallahassee, Florida; Trenton, New Jersey; Tucson, Arizona; and Washington, DC. Many rallies were sponsored by MoveOn.org, in solidarity with the workers of Madison, but several were organized by local activists who wanted to express their support of and extend their solidarity to the protesters in Wisconsin.

Rallies ranged in size from tens to thousands of protesters. They included many union people, as identified by their signs, often their hats or jackets, and sometimes their flags and banners. Sometimes protesters identified themselves by the work they did: teacher, boilermaker, electrician; others by their union: machinists, autoworkers, steelworkers, postal workers, service employees, laborers, and so on.

In some places the rallies were organized by organized labor, such the state AFL-CIO, as in Austin or in Indianapolis; in other places concerned citizens, labor movement supporters, political activists, and the like organized the protests.

Some of these were general solidarity rallies, where people gathered to publicly proclaim their support for the protesters in Madison. The February 21 rally in Baltimore was organized for members of the American Federation of State, County and Municipal Employees (AFSCME) to express their support for their public-sector brothers and sisters in Wisconsin. The February 26 rally at DuPont Circle in Washington, DC, was held to express general solidarity with the people of Wisconsin.

Some workers and unions in other states held rallies to demonstrate publicly that they would not accept similar treatment by their governors. Certainly, rallies in places like Columbus, Indianapolis, Lansing, and Trenton were examples of these, as workers in these states resented being singled out by Republicans and conservative Democrats. Workers in these cities were aware of the attacks on them, as well as the attacks on Wisconsin workers, but they had a certain awareness that this was also happening in other parts of the world, such as North Africa and the Middle East. A sign in Indianapolis summed it up, with wording imposed over a map of the world: "We Stand with Workers of Wisconsin and the World."

And speaking of Indianapolis: while Republican legislators in Indiana were escalating attacks on teachers and labor in general, the Indiana AFL-CIO mobilized thousands of workers on a cold, blustery day. Workers in this largely white but somewhat racially mixed crowd brought back the spirit of the 1960s, using one of the most radical chants of the era to express their opposition to how they were being targeted. During the rally these workers, many apparently quite conservative personally, began to chant spontaneously, "Hell, no, we won't go!"

Some of these protests were more specific—and targeted. According to CNN, one rally on February 22 was held outside the Washington, DC, offices of Governor Scott Walker. Another Washington, DC, rally, on March 16, was held outside a fund-raiser for the Wisconsin GOP. According to an account on *Daily Kos*, the sidewalk was half-filled when the protest began, but then the crowd wrapped around the block, invaded the street, and eventually entered the lobby of the building where the fund-raiser was being held, and the ensuing noise vibrated off the walls.

Comments on this latter protest conveyed people's thinking. There was a real sense of empowerment, that business was not going to continue as usual. Some even saw events such as these as a turning of the tide, wherein progressives, after being subjected to years of right-wing onslaught, now were pushing back. Enthusiasm was high.

These sentiments were reflected in the signs people carried. Some simply identified their organization, which was true of a number of unions, and these were often printed. Some were more traditional union signs, usually printed, often urging, "Save the Middle Class." However, the large majority of signs were handwritten or painted. Many were obscene, especially those focusing on the right-wing Koch brothers, who were major funders of several Wisconsin politicians, including Walker himself. Others were more general: one proclaimed, "Save our public services." And many were specifically anticorporate and often in the context of "us against them," in a generally inchoate but on-target form of emerging class consciousness. Many, if not most, of these signs reflected deep resentment at being targeted for criticism even though workers had not caused the problems, and umbrage that the elites who had caused the problems were, in fact, getting away unscathed.

Such sentiments were also communicated, much more widely, on websites. Many videos were shot at rallies and posted on YouTube to try to convey the experience more fully. By February 21 the Labor Network of the Democratic Socialists of America (DSA) had posted a collection of articles, videos, and responses on its website, including a note from a police officer in western New York who urged protesters to "keep up the good work!" Another responder urged readers to consider labor history, comparing events in Madison with the general strike in San Francisco.

But perhaps the most inspiring video posted on YouTube came from a husband-wife team from Washington State. The man was originally from Wisconsin, and the couple was so inspired by the protests in Madison that they tried to fly in to express their solidarity. But they were grounded by bad weather. So they worked with AFSCME members to build support for people in Wisconsin. They joined others in taking over the state capitol in Olympia while wearing their green AFSCME t-shirts and scarves. The highlight of the occupation was when the crowd sang "On Wisconsin!" in the capitol, although the words had been slightly modified. As the woman noted, "It was incredible!"

People from around the country were talking about events in Madison, communicating what they had experienced or learned. A lively ongoing exchange occurred on the listserv of the United Association for Labor Education (UALE), in which I participated as a member. A few slices give a taste (the authors are not identified since they haven't agreed to such). A labor educator in Nebraska wrote:

> The battle for the hearts and minds of our members and the general public is, at this point, as serious as a heart attack. And I believe that we have ceded the field to those who hate or don't understand organized labor.
>
> … How to get the numbers of our members and their families to understand the crisis, why it's a crisis, and to act in shows of solidarity. Is there any labor educator (union or university) that hasn't heard leaders and activists lament that the "biggest challenge we face is member apathy"?
>
> We have to find ways to help leaders and activists "unionize the organized." What's the message? How is it most effectively delivered? When is it best delivered? …
>
> How to explain the labor movement to "persuadables" in the general public who are not members but have an idea of what unions are and due [sic] thanks to the exaggerations, half-truths, distortions, and ugly anti-union stereotypes that float around in society masquerading as the truth. The public, whether it reads the NYT [*New York Times*] or listens to Fox News, does have an opinion of what unions are and do that is NOT complementary [sic] … What are the best idioms, metaphors, etc. that can be used to explain unions to the general public?

Another member tied the attacks on Wisconsin workers to the wars:

> There is plenty of money out there to solve the fiscal problems of the states— but it is misdirected towards wars abroad and military spending in general.
>
> The VAST yearly sums spent by the Pentagon and routinely approved by our Congressional representatives are more than the combined military spending of all other countries on earth. That is obscene. This in no way negates the contributions of our many brothers and sisters in uniform. But we think there is a better way to peace than constant, escalating warfare.
>
> This is offered in the spirit of solidarity to all our labor educator brothers and sisters and to the trade unionists with which you work.
>
> [My organization is] dedicated to ending the wars in Iraq and Afghanistan and to redirecting that war spending towards jobs and our many domestic needs here in the US.

Another wrote of experiences teaching about these developments:

> I teach in a sociology program [at a university in the Midwest] … My classes are often … students right out of high school, along with non-traditional, older students who have returned to school. My students are rarely progressive … our area is in terrible shape economically—when an Olive Garden opened a couple of years ago, over 2500 people applied to work as waiters … Yesterday, I spent time in each of my four courses to talk about Madison and what's going on.
>
> One of the points I made—and I was consciously taking a fairly restrained approach—was that I don't see how destroying any union is going to help working people. And my students got that.
>
> Because I … see the US in a global context—I was able to talk about what's going on in North Africa and the Middle East, and tie it to Madison … I was also able to tie in the fact … the US is spending over $1 trillion a year for all military-related expenses … and that money spent on the military cannot be spent on college education grants, health care, education in general, infrastructure development, confronting climate change, etc. …
>
> And when I told them about how I was watching "The Ed Show" last Thursday night—Ed Schultz was broadcasting from the Wisconsin State Capitol, and the TV showed that people were relaxed, not being violent or "rioting" or any of that—and then turned to Bill O'Reilly who at the exact same time was claiming that there was a "riot" and "insurrection" at that moment taking place in Madison—well, they all got the idea that they need to be critical consumers of what's in the media.

Among the many who traveled to Madison to express their solidarity, the most inspiring were members of Iraq Veterans Against the War (IVAW), some of whom spent days in the capitol. IVAW members made it a point to talk with members of the Wisconsin National Guard and then publicly asked them to disregard orders from Governor Walker—who was threatening to mobilize them to clear the protesters from the capitol.

IVAW members from across the upper Midwest held their own march in Madison on March 19 in solidarity with the workers of Wisconsin. Members traveled from Indiana, Illinois, Minnesota, and western Colorado to join their comrades from Wisconsin. They were joined by members of Vietnam Veterans Against the War, both from out of state as well as Wisconsin, who provided security for the demonstration. These veterans, men and women, were warmly received as they marched up State Street to the capitol, but where they showed their style was when they identified themselves: they introduced themselves as "My name is _____, and I was a public worker with the U.S. Marine Corps/Army/ Navy/Air Force/National Guard!"

And after a month and a half, part of organized labor flexed its muscle on behalf of the workers in Madison. On April 4, Local 10 of the International Longshore and Warehouse Union (ILWU) shut down the ports of San Francisco and Oakland for twenty-four hours. Interestingly, the leadership wanted to use a provision in the ILWU contract with the Pacific Maritime Association (the West Coast shippers' organization) to shut down the ports for eight hours, but rank-and-file members of the local insisted on staying out twenty-four hours. They held this action on the anniversary of Dr. Martin Luther King's 1968 assassination in Memphis, where he was supporting a strike by public workers.

Even as workers in other states were supporting developments in Wisconsin, developments in Madison were encouraging progressive efforts around the country. Progressives swept all ten executive board positions and forty-five of eighty joint board positions of UAW Local 2865, which includes 12,000 teaching assistants, graduate student instructors, readers, and tutors at the various campuses of the University of California through the affiliated Association of Graduate Student Employees. The executive board of the Chicago Teachers Union (Local 1 of the American Federation of Teachers) reasserted its prerogatives and rescinded a deal that President Karen Lewis had made with state legislators without consulting the board concerning a Illinois Senate bill about so-called education reform. The executive board held Lewis accountable for failing to consult its members even though she had led progressive forces to victory in 2009. (Unfortunately, legislators pushed her agreement with them through and got it signed on the basis of the original agreement.) Labor educators and activists mobilized to successfully defend Don Giljum, an adjunct instructor of labor studies at the University of Missouri at St. Louis, against attacks by the right-wing activist and smear-jockey Andrew Breitbart. The labor journalist Harry Kelber published a series of articles on how to fix the AFL-CIO, in a continuing effort to help stimulate thinking about how to revitalize the labor movement. In Chicago, May Day celebrations were bigger and more elaborate than they had been in a very long time and included a rededication of the monument to the Haymarket martyrs of 1886. In Ohio unions and workers mobilized more than 10,000 people and submitted enough signatures by the end of June to put before voters the question of whether the state should eliminate collective bargaining in the public sector. And at the end of June 2011, despite verbal attacks on public workers by New York's Democratic governor Andrew Cuomo and New Jersey's Republican governor Chris Christie, 45,000 Connecticut state workers rejected a deal that union leaders had negotiated with Democratic governor Dannel Malloy to save $1.6 billion in labor costs, which threw the state's balanced budget plans out the window. At considerable personal risk, these workers refused to passively roll over and play dead when attacked by so-called political allies.

In addition, staff members at the labor activist–oriented journal *Labor Notes* have oriented their annual "troublemaker" schools, essentially seminars aimed at labor activists, to focus on and learn from Madison. They held sessions in Chicago, Los Angeles, and San Francisco in May and June and planned additional sessions in the Twin Cities and Philadelphia in September. I attended the session in Chicago, where the focus was almost entirely on Madison and what could be learned from it; other sessions were devoted to seeing what we could learn from the struggle overall to improve our efforts in the Windy City.

Thus we have seen, during a period in which organized labor supposedly was on the skids, a mass movement emerge from below like a mole and shake up the status quo, first in Wisconsin and then across the United States. It inspired people nationally—especially working people—and in a way that hasn't been seen in forty years.

IMPACT OF WISCONSIN ON WORKERS AROUND THE COUNTRY

What has been Wisconsin's impact on the country? I think it is useful to discuss the immediate and longer-term effects.

Most people have focused on the immediate impact. The mass mobilizations, the militant speeches from the capitol, the targeted protests, and the reporting of them by both mainstream and alternative media—across the state, the nation, and, literally, the world—made people feel proud, made them feel worthy on a public level again, and that gave them hope. I think protesters' actions reflected how they think their unions and organizations *should* act, which is a thinly veiled criticism that they have not been acting as members think they should. That this took place during a period of incredible mobilization and struggle in a number of Arab countries across North Africa and the Middle East—and events in Egypt seemed to resonate deeply—also made Wisconsin workers conscious of a broader connection with the peoples of the world in a way perhaps not felt since Vietnam.

The solidarity generated—not only among people in Madison but with people in Madison—was inspiring, and it connected people in ways that much of the labor movement does not and cannot. This emotional response transcended much of the rationality of day-to-day operations, and while it could not last long, its emergence signified a great longing for connection and collectivity. Feelings of solidarity need to be addressed, as they are missing from the lives of many Americans.

While I do not want to negate or minimize the positive, immediate effects of what happened in Wisconsin, I think the long-term impact ultimately will be more important. What did we learn?

First, working people can be mobilized when they understand the issues—especially when they are directly attacked—and when leadership inspires them beyond immediate self-interest. This requires leaders to have a broad vision of social justice and to be willing to stand up unapologetically for the good of workers and the larger community.

Second, workers will join with other like-minded organizations and individuals in a collective manner when they see that their interests and concerns are not dismissed or denigrated but are seen as contributing to the overall good of society.

Third, despite all the demonization of labor in recent decades by the right wing and most of the mainstream mass media, as well as by many conservative Democrats, nonunion people will support workers and their issues when workers mobilize for social justice. Nonunion people recognize that the labor movement contributes to the well-being of all, not just its own members.

Both unionized workers and their allies will respond to visionary leadership when it is respectful while being inspiring, and when it directly asserts its goals, its values, and its demands for justice.

In short, labor must internally confront its, shall we say, less than progressive history (its reactionary history, some might argue) since the 1950s and change its focus from business to social justice. By doing so, as Wisconsin demonstrates, labor can regain its place of leadership alongside other leading social justice organizations and help lead struggles for a better world. Working people can again be shown to have progressive values and be worthy of support and alliances. In other words, Wisconsin has shown labor the path to the future—if only it will reject its recent past of inward self-indulgence.

These are important lessons. They require union leaders to contemplate two more questions: How do we prepare workers for future struggles? And how do we convince workers to join unions, both to increase their power in their various workplaces and to begin to revitalize the labor movement?

The point is that these struggles are not over. The attacks on collective bargaining are really efforts to continue weakening unions, thus making them even less able to resist attacks in the future. But the struggle extends beyond defending collective bargaining, as important as that is. The attacks are on efforts to provide fair pay and social services to members; ultimately, the right wing would like to just dismantle any services not provided by private businesses while destroying unions in the private sector. Those of us who are being attacked need to recognize that this really is an attack on self-governance: the powers-that-be want to tell us how to live, while giving us minimal resources by which to do so, and they don't want our opinions—only our labor power. We've each got to decide whether this is how we want to live—and what kind of labor movement we will leave our children and grandchildren.

What I saw on my two trips to Madison was that people there had already started asking questions that went beyond collective bargaining: How can we establish organizations and institutions to govern ourselves in ways that advance our interests instead of allowing them to be sidelined or turned against us? Frankly, that is a question that labor union officials were trying desperately to stuff back into the bottle—we can't think beyond collective bargaining or the Democrats!—but it is clear that a growing number of people in Wisconsin are asking questions such as this.

And this might be the most important impact of the protests in Wisconsin.

The upsurge in Wisconsin has been inspiring, in the state, nationally, and even in Cairo. It was a catalyst for activists, especially those in the labor movement. Many have been and will be moved in good directions by it.

Yet, as I have argued, we have much to learn from these struggles, both positive and negative. We need to celebrate the positive while mining the negative: we need to address the roots of the upsurge and build organizations that will not only help stimulate future confrontations but advance the struggle for global economic and social justice.

FURTHER READING

Scipes, Kim, "10,000 Join Iraq Veterans in Madison March and Rally," *The Veteran*, Vol. 41 (Spring 2011).

Street, Paul, "Beyond the Ballot Mania: Wisconsin Reflections," *Z Net*, Aug. 14, 2011.

Wang, Dan S., and Nicolas Lampert, "Wisconsin's Lost Strike Moment," Just Seeds Artists Cooperative, Apr. 21, 2011.

16 WISCONSIN IS GLOBAL: THE SHAPE OF THINGS TO COME

By Ashok Kumar and Simon Hardy

After the 2008 credit crunch, a new phase of global capitalism emerged, marked by austerity, attacks on the democratic process and civil rights—and the emergence of mass movements of resistance. Analogies with radical points in history, such as 1968, 1919, or 1848, must always be used with caution, but there are similarities. The acute consciousness of the protest movements and the feeling of unity in struggle, of not being on one's own, are common to all these turning points in history. The first three months of 2011 saw numerous fronts of struggle break out around the world against austerity measures and antidemocratic actions of governments. In many places the public became radicalized in reaction to the violence or austerity regimes of state power and shook the ground beneath the power structure.

The defiance by the people of Wisconsin occurred in the context of a global assault on working people and an upsurge of resistance from below. From each vantage point in the global village we see the resistance movements of others through a variety of lenses and prisms, each one seen and understood against historical examples and present-day struggles. Activists within a movement may find it difficult to imagine that what they are doing is important to people in other countries who are watching live demonstrations on the Internet or following the activists in other ways. Twitter feeds, Facebook, and the "virtual marches" in which anyone can participate without leaving the bedroom seem to take this logic even further. We experience the protests and dissent of others, even in a virtual way.

The story of Madison has been retold around the world: a city of just more than 200,000 people that erupted in protest, with citizens occupying the state capitol for weeks and holding rallies that attracted more than 100,000. The scale of the movement—its size, shape, and militancy rising from the heartland of the nation—prompted global astonishment as the movement was sustained. The story of Wisconsin was not viewed in isolation. The austerity measures and budget crises in Wisconsin were ripped straight from the neoliberal playbook. Across Europe and the United States, bailouts of the financial sector incurred debt that was to be repaid through cuts to welfare, health care, and education.

Wisconsin governor Scott Walker's budget legislation was part of the longer trend of US decline. The heady economic boom days of the 1950s and 1960s are gone, as are the expansionary Clinton years (the globalization bubble). Now that the United States is beset on all sides by increased competition, by its overaccumulation of debt and over-production of various commodities, stagnant industries and structural unemployment are blocking the restoration of prosperity, and things don't look so good. The most dynamic sector of the US economy, as well as that of Britain, is among the most parasitic and unproductive of the economic sectors: finance; this sector also contributes dangerous financial practices to the world market. This was the context for the uprising in Wisconsin, as well as the mass strikes in Spain, Greece, and France; the occupation of Millbank Towers in London; and, of course, the Arab revolutions. The notorious bill in Wisconsin was part of a larger attack, an effort to reconfigure the political power of the state and society that was taking place internationally.

It is important to note that the spirit of rebellion against a global system was evident in the signs and symbols of the Wisconsin move-ment that reached around the world. Images of Madison's occupied capitol could be found on the streets of major cities in Europe. Madison's story was woven into local chants, banners, and struggles, confirming to those in postindustrialized countries that Americans were resist-ing the neoliberal attack. During Britain's largest trade union protest in decades, repeated chants of "London, Cairo, Wisconsin, we will fight, we will win," echoed down the streets of London in March 2011, drawing direct links between these diverse struggles. By June, journal-ists covering the mass strikes in the United Kingdom were describing "Wisconsin-on-the-Thames."

In Madison, likewise, protesters held placards that connected their struggle to the resistance in Egypt. Many compared Scott Walker to

Hosni Mubarak. Is it ridiculous to compare a thirty-year dictator with a democratically elected Republican governor?

What really links the apparently diverse movements of resistance is their parallel existence at a particular conjuncture of world political and economic history. From this flows a whole new struggle involving both progressive and reactionary forces. Our goal in this essay is to describe the fundamental causes of resistance from Wisconsin to Cairo, from the streets of Spain to those of Greece, and the particular sociological and political dynamics that they demonstrate.

THE POLITICAL AND THE ECONOMIC

Madison and Cairo were the sites of movements that were ostensibly about democratic rights. At issue in Egypt was the right to vote and enjoy free political association, while in Madison the focus was on the right to collective bargaining and to exercise basic trade union rights, a symbol of the larger protective social network. The demand that ruling groups fulfill their obligations set the stage, and the political or military leaders refused to give back the rights they had stolen. That said, the movement in Wisconsin followed a different trajectory than that in Tahrir Square.

In Wisconsin, the detonator of the protests was the imposition of new antiunion legislation. The Wisconsin struggle was truly a social movement because it drew in wider sections of the population that found common cause with union members in the fight over union rights and against austerity. In this sense the struggle became a generalized political struggle against Walker and everything he represents—social inequality, bully-boy politics, and the growing power of the right-wing axis comprised of the Republican Party and the Tea Party movement.

In Egypt, meanwhile, the movement returned to the socioeconomic as a crucial realization of the heightened level of struggle needed to overthrow Mubarak. The systemic poverty and social alienation that mark the lives of millions across the Middle East ordinarily would have left Mohammed Bouazizi, a small business owner, just another anonymous victim of capitalist globalization. His self-immolation gave birth to the uprising in Tunisia, which then spread to Egypt and beyond. This uprising was a demand for elementary rights; it represented the unfulfilled promise of the French Revolution, the demands of the modern-day *sans-culottes* and lower middle class to engage in public political life. This was the unfinished dream of the Jacobins, a mass movement composed of many classes and interests, under the leadership of forces demanding democratic rights rather than dramatic social change.

The occupation of Tahrir Square was an act of reconstituting civil society in the process of struggling against a dictatorship. Social demands were the foundation for further action. Demands for political change—such as the right to vote, the right to assemble, the right to elect political leaders—constituted a direct attempt by ordinary people to regain control of their lives and their economy. The urgent task is to find a synthesis of the economic and political on an international and a national level.

NEW TACTICS

Clearly the tactic of occupation has become a central weapon in activists' arsenal and a global symbol of resistance today. Whether the occupation is of a central city square, the headquarters of a ruling party, or the capitol in Wisconsin, the tactic demonstrates the mobilization of civil society against the oppressive state and economic elites. It is a partially symbolic, partially practical, manifestation of the *citizen* in a physical assault on institutions and geographical spaces of power. On the same February day that the people of Tahrir Square celebrated the news of Mubarak's resignation, Walker announced the introduction of his "budget repair" bill. Spurred by a determination to protest the budget bill, the Wisconsin labor movement and its allies occupied the capitol. The attempt to take part in a nominally democratic process became something more.

The occupation of Tahrir Square itself was of particular symbolic importance. *Tahrir* means liberation in Arabic; the square is in the center of downtown Cairo, and demonstrations there were forbidden under the British occupation and subsequent dictatorships. Taking Tahrir and holding it in the face of terrible police violence and the threat of a massacre by the army were necessary to give the revolution a focal point, as well as a vocal point—a place where the masses could be seen and recognized by their size and anger. Some initially argued that Tahrir Square was inspired by earlier revolutions that have brought down various dictators or anti-Western political regimes in the new century. But those were very much products of the westward-looking middle classes, organized by activist groups with connections to various Washington think tanks. Egypt experienced a truly popular uprising that upset the Washington experts badly and left them scrambling to try to regain ground. The occupation of Tahrir Square was actually an act of defiance against the West and against the West's favorite dictator, and a demand for Egypt to be ruled democratically for the first time in its history.

The political-economic bases of the struggle and the similarity of tactics are clear in the Spanish movement that emerged first in Madrid and then spread across Spain. Initially a project of nongovernmental organizations of the quasi-Left, the Spanish movement quickly attracted a cast of largely young people demanding "real democracy now!" in the face of an increasingly unpopular social democratic government that was implementing huge cuts across the public sector. In a country where youth unemployment is about 40 percent, it could not have been a surprise when the dispossessed and the alienated were inspired by the occupation of Tahrir Square and what Egyptians achieved there.

Tahrir has, in fact, a growing brood of political children around the world. The various city-center occupations challenged capitalism and demanded greater social equality. In so doing, they became the central focus of the news cycle as young activists found a voice to express their discontent with what life in Spain, for instance, had failed to provide for them. A similar camp was set up in Syntagma Square in Athens, organized by the *aganaktismenoi* (outraged), and activists began to discuss the activities among other camps in other cities across the continent. But what to demand?

VIOLENCE AND RESISTANCE

Despite the clear value of occupations, this tactic can have its limitations and can even sometimes lead to disastrous outcomes if the struggle does not spread beyond the immediate locality. Brave prodemocracy movements failed at Tiananmen in 1989 and Bangkok in 2009, for example. This points to another common feature of the struggles: the role of force or threat of force. The use of force in the United States could not be the same as that applied by the trained torturers of Mubarak's secret police—and, indeed, the popularity of the Wisconsin resistance depended on its absolute nonviolence, which was even commended by friendly local police. But perhaps the strategies of violence of those actually in power in both the West and the East are not so different after all.

In Greece riot police repeatedly attacked the occupiers of Syntagma Square during the protest. Syntagma was a popular movement that explicitly rejected International Monetary Fund loans, the associated structural adjustment program, and the weakness of the Papandreou government in standing up to the dictatorship of international financiers. The pan-European financial and legal mechanisms of the European Union raised questions of national sovereignty and self-determination, causing both a nationalist spasm in countries contributing to bailout ("Why are we helping the Greeks, Portuguese, or Irish?") and a desire to resist the impositions of the European central bank. But more than this, running through everything was the feeling of being disempowered by shadowy financial institutions that were effectively blackmailing whole countries. Syntagma, as much as Tahrir and Puerto del Sol, represents a desire to free the individual from bureaucracy, from the sheriff and the bank manager. When the Greek government passed its austerity budget by only five votes in late June 2011, and with 80 percent of Greeks opposed, the insurmountable chasm between those in power and the people they supposedly represent was clear. Challenges to what protesters regard as undemocratic practices by politicians are met with violence, in a clear reaffirmation by the state that, "Yes, what we are doing is unpopular, but you cannot be allowed to stop us."

What is striking in the age of globalization is progressive forces' international experience that resistance to police is met by state violence. The popular slogan "This is what democracy looks like" can be heard from the Wisconsin Capitol to Tahrir Square to the Puerta del Sol Square in Madrid. Mass mobilization and resistance offer people more real and direct control over their lives than parliamentary democracy or a dictatorship ever could. The opposition has not yet articulated a clear vision of an alternative.

POLITICIANS: SAME SUITS, DIFFERENT NAME

What about the relationship between the politicians and the resistance movement? Every country has politicians who arrogantly bare their teeth and those who carry out austerity measures with a sorry shake of the head. The abandonment of the Wisconsin Senate by the "Fab 14" state senators was not altogether an act of courage but a combination of bold actions by some senators and a desperate act by others who might have supported cutbacks (as Democrats did in other states) but who were caught between competing interests. For the latter, running away appeared to be the only option—on their return, these state senators were especially eager to see the mass movement dispersed. If the uprising encouraged them to envision their own political renaissance, it also rattled them.

In Egypt the ruling National Democratic Party enjoyed a permanent and unmediated relationship with the institutions of power. The movement against Mubarak had few friends in high places within the country itself, if many unreliable friends abroad. The intervention by the United States was designed to slow down or even frustrate a transition to democracy while demanding the prodemocracy movement limit itself in the face of brutal state repression. The arrival of ElBaradei as a potential president-in-waiting was greeted warmly by the West. Co-optation, often the last resort, can also be the most effective. The political elite of Egypt pitted the military and police against the people, while in Wisconsin the exemption of some unions from the suspension of collective bargaining rights was intended to calm the public. Then the firefighters joined the protest, and local police showed their sympathy. From that point on, Wisconsin saw an ever-growing, ever-strengthening sense of solidarity from farmer to health worker to teacher to firefighter. Unionists and others arriving from out of state were met with grateful enthusiasm and echoes of "thank you, thank you!"

Movements of resistance must find allies wherever they can. But around the world, activists have begun to learn painful lessons about who is trustworthy and who is not. The protests by British students against government cuts and the trebling of tuition fees in October 2010 were the largest in a generation. The students who took to the streets were fighting back against education's becoming more of what it already was. There, one of the primary causes of the student uprising was the feeling of betrayal by the Liberal Democrats, junior partner in the ruling coalition, who had promised to campaign to scrap tuition fees and vote against any increase. Since the election, they, too, promoted a threefold increase in fees. The Labour Party, which many trade unionists still regarded as their party, adopted a hostile attitude toward the public-sector strikes of June 30 and inflicted harsher words on the teachers and civil servants than the financial sector ever had to hear.

THE POLITICAL STRUGGLE WITHIN THE MOVEMENT

The same is true of trade union leaders almost everywhere. The trade unions play a crucial role in the fight against austerity measures internationally, since their members see their unions as the first line of defense against job cuts or wage slashing. Union leaders perform a perpetual balancing act: seeking to keep members happy, or at least satisfied, while dampening the resistance and strikes sure to unsettle their own legitimacy. National leaders in the AFL-CIO called for two "lobby days," with little apparent intention of putting up a real fight, hoping instead that Democrats will sweep elections for seats in the legislature in 2012—although some of these union leaders gamely showed up personally in Madison, in some cases offering money to support the protests and rallying their members outside the state to the Wisconsin cause. State and local labor leaders within Wisconsin acted better, in some cases much better—but still were unable to catch up with the movement. All this tended to create a vacuum in effective leadership. Unionists and the best of their leaders did not simply come to the rallies at the capitol steps, listen to speeches, and go home. This time was different; this time they returned by the tens, hundreds, and thousands —or stayed.

This interaction of the movement with the establishment is a crucial nexus at which competing interests and agencies engage in an often concealed but sometimes open struggle. The establishment wants to contain, limit, demobilize, and break up the movement through a panoply of tactics, including demoralization, co-optation, or outright suppression. In Egypt the prodemocracy movement had a fraught and fragile relationship with the Muslim Brotherhood, which also played a conservative role within the struggles.

While the great mass of Brotherhood members are certainly committed to reforms that might be Islamic in character or simply express a desire for something different, the leadership cynically manipulated the movement to position itself for the new order, post-Mubarak. After Mubarak fell (and his departure, of course, was only the first stage of the revolution, not the last), the Muslim Brotherhood joined the clarion calls by the military and the international community to end the Tahrir Square protests and for the striking workers to return to their jobs. The urgent demand of Brotherhood elites for normality, another word for counterrevolution, was raised against the urgent need to disrupt the normal running of affairs in order to force greater change. Normality became their watchword. They played a loyal role in securing a victory in the subsequent referendum, which acted to undermine the democratic aspirations of the people.

In the movements that emerge against neoliberalism, austerity campaigns, and dictatorships, the relationship between the radically democratic urges of ordinary people and the conservative responses of existing leaderships or institutions is ripe for rupture.

QUESTIONS OF POWER

The realization of politics proper within a supposedly postideological world is a terrifying thought for virtually the entire political class. The political machine swings into action, urging the limitation of the struggle to minimal reforms. There is a fear, a veritable specter, that stalks the global ruling elites: the specter of mass, sustained unrest, if not something worse. The fear is that any serious struggle by working people, youth, the urban poor, and impoverished immigrants—in short, the dispossessed at large—will follow the logical progression of ideas to challenging the power structures and social relations that exist within the supposed democratic framework.

What is really being challenged is the power of the rich, the bankocracy, the governments, the military—remember, the central plank of the Thatcherite counterreforms in Britain in the 1980s was the "right to manage" (i.e., the right of capital to dominate in all decisions). Today, the upper class fights for the right to continue profiteering while making the majority pay for the economic crisis. Of course, this right of *this* minority is incompatible with our aspirations and how we understand our democratic and social rights as a majority, which is why the elites must undermine and attack these rights and reinforce their own. In Britain coordinated strikes on June 30, 2011, in protest of cuts to pension provisions for public-sector workers, were met with the threat of passage of more antiunion laws to ban coordinated action (political strikes and solidarity strikes are already banned).

Inevitably, within the resistance movements that emerge around our democratic rights and the socioeconomic questions of debt and who pays, there will be disagreements about how to fight and how to win. Across the Arab world people want to get rid of the regimes and bring in something more democratic—but what? In Spain the youth in Madrid and Barcelona called for real democracy (not tomorrow but now!), but who could clearly delineate what this was? Many proposed alternatives were in fact variations of what already existed.

What we are all grappling with is power: who has it, who wants it, how to fight it, and what to do with it. Things are likely to get worse before they get better. Certainly, the increasingly popular view is that people want power over their own lives, and they are angry at the Walkers, Mubaraks, Assads, Camerons, and Zapateros of this world. What people internationally express is disillusionment with what they have and the desire to find something new, a new form and content for our societies and lives.

What comes after the Walkers and Mubaraks is yet to be determined, but what we can see is the necessity for increasing resistance. More people are coming to see that the ideological claim of globalization as the answer to all problems proved problematic, perhaps irretrievably. Maybe now, radically democratic alternatives, unimaginable even in 2006, can be devised and seriously debated. If we accept that we need power in the hands of ordinary people rather than the ruling groups, then the task is to find ways to do that through the organization of resistance and international solidarity.

FURTHER READING

Bailey, Michael, and Des Freedman, eds, *The Assault on Universities: A Manifesto for Resistance*, London: Pluto, 2011.

Solomon, Clare, and Tania Palmieri, eds, *Springtime: The New Student Rebellions*, New York: Verso, 2011.

AFTERWORD: HOW I GOT TO MADISON

By Michael Moore

About 1 a.m. I finished work for the day on my current project (top secret for now—sorry, no spoiler alerts!). That was when I clicked on the link someone had sent me to a discussion Bill O'Reilly had had with Sarah Palin a few hours earlier about my belief that in the twenty-first century the money of the rich really isn't theirs—and that a vast chunk of it should be taken away from them.

O'Reilly and Palin were referring to comments I had made earlier in the week on a small cable show called *GRITtv*. I honestly didn't know this was going to air that night (I had been asked to stop by and say a few words of support for a nurses' union video), but I spoke from my heart about the millions of our fellow Americans who have had their homes and jobs stolen from them by a criminal class of millionaires and billionaires. It was the morning after the Oscars, during which the winner of Best Documentary for *Inside Job* stood at the microphone and declared, "I must start by pointing out that three years after our horrific financial crisis caused by financial fraud, not a single financial executive has gone to jail. And that's wrong." And he was applauded for saying this. (When did they stop booing Oscar speeches? Damn!)

So *GRITtv* ran my comments—and all week the right-wing-opoly was upset by what I said: that the money that the rich have stolen (or not paid taxes on) belongs to the American people. Drudge-Limbaugh-Beck and even Donald Trump went nuts, calling me names and suggesting I move to Cuba.

So in the wee hours of the morning I sat down to write an answer to them. By 3 a.m. it had turned into more of a manifesto of class war—or, I should say, a manifesto against the class war the rich have been conducting against the American people for thirty years. I read it aloud to myself to see how it sounded (trying not to wake anyone else in the apartment) and then—and this is why no one should be up at 3 a.m.— the crazy kicked in: I needed to get in the car and drive to Madison and give this speech.

I went online to get directions and saw that no official big rally was planned like the one they had the previous week and the one scheduled for the next week. Just the normal ongoing demonstration and occupation of the state capitol that had been in process since February 12 (the day after Mubarak was overthrown in Egypt) to protest the Republican governor's move to kill the state's public unions.

So, it's three in the morning and I'm a thousand miles from Madison, and I see that the open microphone for speakers starts at noon. Hmm. No time to drive from New York. So I was off to the airport. I left a note on the kitchen table saying I'd be back at 9 p.m. Called a friend and asked him if he wanted to meet me at the Delta counter. Called the guy who manages my website, woke him up, and asked him to track down the coordinators in Madison and tell them I'm on my way and would like to say a few words, if possible—"but tell them if they've got other plans or no room for me, I'll be happy just to stand there holding a sign and singing 'Solidarity Forever.' "

So I just show up. The firefighters, hearing I'm there, ask me to lead their protest parade through downtown Madison. I march with them, along with John Nichols (who lives in Madison and writes for the *Nation*). Congresswoman Tammy Baldwin and the great singer Michelle Shocked show up.

The scene in Madison is nothing like what they are showing you on TV or in the newspaper. First, you notice that the whole town is behind this. Yard signs and signs in store windows are everywhere, supporting public workers. Thousands of people are out, just randomly lining the streets for the six blocks leading to the capitol, and carrying signs, shouting, and cheering and cajoling. Then there are stages and friendly competing demos on all sides of the building (the estimate for the day before was 50,000 to 70,000 people, the smallest one yet!). Jim Hoffa of the Teamsters had sent a semi, and it is parked like a don't-even-think-of-effing-with-us Sherman tank on the street in front of the capitol. There is a long line—separate from the other demonstrations—of 4,000 people, waiting their turn to get through the only open door to the capitol so they can join the occupation inside.

And inside the rotunda is … well, it would bring tears to your eyes if you saw it. It was like a shrine to working people—to what America is and should be about—packed with families and kids and so many senior citizens that it made me happy for science and its impact on life expectancy over the past century. There were grandmas and great-grandpas who remember FDR and Wisconsin's La Follette and the long view of this struggle. Standing in that rotunda was like a religious experience. There had been nothing like it, for me, in decades.

And so it was in this setting, out of doors now on the steps of the capitol, with so many people in front of me that I couldn't see where they ended, that I just showed up and gave a speech that felt unlike any other I had ever given. Because I had just written it and had no time to memorize it, I read from the pages I brought with me. I wanted to make sure that the words I had chosen were clear and exact. I knew they had the potential to drive the haters into a rabid state (not a pretty sight), but I also feared that the Right's wealthy patrons would see a need to retaliate, should these words be met with citizen action across the land. I was, after all, putting them on notice: We are coming after you, we are stopping you, and we are going to return the money/jobs/homes you stole from people. You have gone too far. It's too bad you couldn't have been satisfied with making millions, you had to have billions—and now you want to strip us of our ability to talk and bargain and provide. This is your tipping point, Wall Street; your come-to-Jesus moment, Corporate America. And I'm glad I'm going to be able to be a witness to it.

You can find the written version of my speech on my website (www.michaelmoore.com). Please read it and pass it around far and wide. You can also find a video on the website of me giving the speech from the capitol steps.

I can't express enough the level of admiration I have for the people of Wisconsin who, for three weeks, braved the brutal winter cold and took over their state capitol. All told, literally hundreds of thousands of people made their way to Madison so their voices could be heard. It all began with high school students cutting class and marching on the building (you can read their reports on my High School Newspaper site, www.mikeshighschoolnews.com). Then their parents joined them. Then fourteen brave Democratic state senators left the state so the governor wouldn't have his quorum.

And all the while the White House was trying to stop this movement.

But it didn't matter. The people's train had left the station. And now protests were springing up in all fifty states.

The media did a poor job covering this (imagine a takeover of the government HQ in any other country, free or totalitarian—our media would be all over it). But this one scared them and their masters—as it should have. The organizers told me later that my showing up got them more coverage than they would have had, "a shot in the arm that we needed to keep momentum going." Well, I'm glad I could help. But they need a lot more than just me—and they need you doing similar things in your own states and towns.

How 'bout it? I know you know this: This is our moment. Let's seize it. Everyone can do something.

P.S. Full disclosure: I am a proud member of four unions: the Directors Guild, Writers Guild, Screen Actors Guild, and the American Federation of Television and Radio Artists (the last two have passed resolutions supporting the workers in Wisconsin). My production company has signed contracts with five unions (and soon there will be a sixth). All my full-time employees have full medical and dental insurance with *no* deductible. So, yes, I'm biased.

POSTSCRIPT: FROM WISCONSIN TO WALL STREET AND BACK

Widely read Firedoglake blogger David Dayen wrote that despite the setbacks the Wisconsin movement experienced, its energy and spirit could be discerned in the Occupy Wall Street protest.

"Both occupations created miniature communities on site … both had young people in the forefront, with medical stations, food areas, communications platforms and general assemblies to hold meetings," Dayen added. Wisconsin had established a pattern spreading, by the second week of October 2011, across the nation.

Wisconsin icons—from plastic cheeseheads to t-shirts depicting the state's borders as a fist—could be seen from Lower Manhattan to Washington, DC. There were even pizza deliveries: Ian's Pizza of Madison had made slices the "nosh of choice," another reporter quipped. The *Nation*'s John Nichols put it even better, calling Occupy America the "protest movement that borrows a page from the Wisconsin protests and takes their focus and passion to the belly of the beast."

99% 99%

OCCUPY MADISON
THROW THE BOSSES OFF YOUR BACK!

FACEBOOK.COM/OCCUPY MADISON • TWITTER:@OCCUPYMADISON99

ACKNOWLEDGMENTS AND CONTRIBUTORS

We wish to thank our friends at Verso for seeing this book from manuscript to print, especially Andrew Hsiao and Mark Martin, and thanks to our excellent copy-editor Polly Kummel. We wish also to thank Cat Warren, editor of *Academe*, the magazine of the American Association of University Professors, for urging the editors to write the essay that sparked this larger project. Special thanks to Danny Goldberg, for help with Tom Morello, and to Bob Mahlenkamp and Henry Haslach, Jr., for advice on the Teaching Assistants' Strike of 1970.

CONTRIBUTORS

PATRICK BARRETT is Administrative Director of the A. E. Havens Center for the Study of Social Structure and Social Change and an instructor in the Latin American, Caribbean and Iberian Studies Program at the University of Wisconsin-Madison.

MARY BOTTARI is the Director of the Center for Media and Democracy's Real Economy Project and works on the CMD websites PRWatch.org, Sourcewatch.org and BanksterUSA.org.

MARI JO BUHLE is an Emerita Professor of History and American Civilization at Brown University, retired to Madison, Wisconsin.

PAUL BUHLE, formerly a Senior Lecturer at Brown University, is also retired to Madison, where he produces radical comics.

ROGER BYBEE edited the weekly *Racine Labor,* 1979–93, and served as Communications Director of three statewide pro-labor organizations. He is a freelance writer based in Milwaukee.

RUTH CONNIFF is the Political Editor of the *Progressive*. In 2011, the editors of *Madison Magazine* named Conniff's coverage of the crisis in Wisconsin the "Best in Madison."

GARY DUMM, a comic artist and long-time collaborator with the late Harvey Pekar, drew large portions of *Students for a Democratic Society: A Graphic History*, and has contributed widely to other comic art anthologies.

SIMON HARDY is a spokesperson for the National Campaign Against Fees and Cuts (NCAFC) in the UK, a student at Westminster University and a member of the group Workers' Power.

FRANK EMSPAK, emeritus faculty, UW School for Workers, is currently the producer of Workers Independent News (WIN), headquartered in Madison.

ASHOK KUMAR is a former Dane County Supervisor (District 5) and was the Education Officer of the London School of Economics Students' Union during the height of the UK student unrest in 2010.

MICHAEL FRANCIS MOORE, a filmmaker, author and progressive-radical commentator on politics, has written and occasionally starred in documentary films. He directed and produced *Bowling for Columbine, Fahrenheit 9/11, Sicko*, and *Capitalism: A Love Story*.

TOM MORELLO, the lead guitarist of Rage Against the Machine, now records under the name Tom Morello: The Nightwatchman. His most recent album is *World Wide Rebel Songs*.

JOHN NICHOLS is Associate Editor of *The Capital Times*, a columnist for the *The Wisconsin State Journal* and Madison.Com, Washington Correspondent and frequent contributor to the *Nation*, and cofounder with Robert McChesney of freepress.net. He is author of *The Genius of*

Impeachment, The Death and Life of American Journalism, and *The "S" Word*, among other books.

DAVID POKLINKOWSKI is a member of the Executive Board of the South Central Federation of Labor, has been President and Business Manager of IBEW Local 2304 in Madison since 1985, and has been Secretary of the Utility Workers Coalition—a coalition of utility unions from across the Midwest—since 1992.

MATTHEW ROTHSCHILD has worked at *The Progressive* since 1983 and has been the editor since 1984. He is the author of *You Have No Rights: Stories of America in an Age of Repression* and the editor of *Democracy in Print: The Best of The Progressive Magazine, 1909–2009.*

SHARON RUDAHL, an art editor of the Madison alternative weekly *Takeover*, has contributed widely to comic art anthologies, wrote and drew *A Dangerous Woman: The Graphic Biography of Emma Goldman.*

CHARITY A. SCHMIDT is a PhD student in Sociology at the University of Wisconsin-Madison. She is an active member of the Teaching Assistants' Association (TAA) and continues to organize with various community groups in the ongoing Wisconsin struggle.

KIM SCIPES is an Associate Professor of Sociology at Purdue University North Central in Westville, Indiana, and Chair of the Chicago Chapter of the National Writers Union. His latest book is *AFL-CIO's Secret War against Developing Country Workers: Solidarity or Sabotage?*

NICK THORKELSON, the first Underground Comix artist in Madison, drew *The Underhanded History of the USA* and illustrated *The Earth Belongs to the People.*